TELLING TALES in English

Photocopiable stories and activities for young learners

By Wendy Superfine and Megan James

DELTA PUBLISHING

Ernst Klett Sprachen
Stuttgart

Contents

	Language	Photocopiable activities	Page
The Leopard's Drum			**10/11**
Lesson 1	*What's this? Can I have ...? Can you lend me?* Animal vocabulary: *elephant, leopard, monkey, python, tortoise*	Shadow puppets	12, 13 14/15
Lesson 2	Story comprehension Animal vocabulary	Worksheet: matching pictures to speech bubbles, crossword puzzle	16, 17
Lesson 3	Adjectives: *small, huge, big, tiny* Superlatives: *smallest, biggest*	Worksheet: writing and drawing	18, 19
Lesson 4	*Can I have ...?* Story vocabulary	Happy families card game	20, 21
Lesson 5	*Can you lend me ...?* Classroom objects: *pencil, pen rubber, ruler, book, crayon, chair, table desk, bag, sharpener, scissors*	Card guessing game	22, 23
The Old Woman who Lived in a Bottle			**24/25**
Lesson 1	Past tense verbs: *had/was* *There is/are, What's the matter?* Story vocabulary	Making a story book	26, 27
Lesson 2	Story vocabulary Story comprehension	Adding speech bubbles to story books	28, 29
Lesson 3	House and furniture vocabulary	Wordsearch	30, 31
Lesson 4	Directions: *go upstairs, turn left/right, go straight on, go up/through/into, go past/down, climb up* Castle vocabulary	Maze puzzle	32, 33
Lesson 5	*want/don't want* *Where is/ where are?* rooms/ furniture vocabulary	Picture dictation	34, 35
The Rich Man and the Shoemaker			**36/37**
Lesson 1	Present tense verbs Present tense questions Story vocabulary	Worksheet: reading comprehension	38, 39
Lesson 2	Story vocabulary	Bingo game	40, 41
Lesson 3	*Where is ...?* Prepositions: *in, on, under, behind, next to, between* Ordinals: *1st, 2nd, 3rd, 4th*	Worksheet: listening and drawing	42, 43
Lesson 4	Present tense verbs: *sing, count, hide, spell* Numbers 1-40	Boardgame	44, 45
Lesson 5	Bedtime routines, *must*	Class survey	46, 47

	Language	Photocopiable activities	Page
The Farmer, his Son and the Donkey			**48/49**
Lesson 1	Present continuous: *sitting, walking, riding, playing, going, carrying* *What is he/are they doing?* Story vocabulary	Snap card game	50, 51
Lesson 2	Present continuous tense Story vocabulary Questions: *What is he/are they doing?*	Worksheet: matching pictures to captions, sequencing card game	52, 53
Lesson 3	Present continuous tense	Spot the differences	54, 55
Lesson 4	Adjectives: *young, strong, big, heavy, sad, happy*	Story book	56, 57
Lesson 5	Comparatives of adjectives: *bigger, stronger, younger, heavier, sadder*	Worksheet: listening and drawing	58, 59
The Honey Pot			**60/61**
Lesson 1	Story vocabulary, Past tense Numbers 1-12	Jumbled sentences	62, 63
Lesson 2	*What do you like? Do you like ...?* Food vocabulary: *milk, honey, bread, cheese*	Breakfast survey Chant	64, 65
Lesson 3	Present tense: *give, has/have, loves, fill, put, try, know* Story vocabulary	Story wheel	66, 67
Lesson 4	Regular past tense verbs: *lived, loved, looked, opened, filled, watched, emptied, tasted, arrived, stared, asked, smiled, nodded, waited, shouted*	Honey pot game	68, 69
Lesson 5	Food vocabulary, *had/was*, Ordinals: *1st, 2nd, 3rd*	Picture dictation	70, 71
The Pied Piper			**72/73**
Lesson 1	Story vocabulary Irregular past tense Present tense: *fight, scratch, bite, eat, run, get*	Chant Picture/word card game	74, 75
Lesson 2	Town places Verbs: *ran, got, fell* Prepositions: *through, over, past, around*	Worksheet: completing maps	76, 77
Lesson 3	Story vocabulary Regular past tenses: *followed, played* Irregular past tenses: *fell, took, came, wore, was, were, ate, had*	Worksheet: putting pictures in order Find a partner game	78, 79
Lesson 4	Irregular past tenses	Verb bingo Gap fill exercise	80, 81
Lesson 5	Past tenses, *There was/were*, Places vocabulary, Numbers 1-15	Memory game	82, 83

General Introduction

Welcome to *Telling Tales in English*, a Delta Publishing resource book and cassette, aimed at teachers of young learners of English aged between 8 and 11 years. This book contains 6 Photocopiable Stories, each accompanied by 5 Photocopiable Lessons and 5 pages of Teacher's Notes. The accompanying cassette contains recordings of the stories, listening texts, songs and chants.

Children hear stories from an early age in their own culture and these stories provide a rich source of motivating material for use in the English classroom.

The stories included here are traditional folk tales, which have been adapted to suit the language ability and interest of the target age group. The 30 Photocopiable Lessons contain a wide variety of activities which practise specific language and vocabulary. While young children are keen to learn, and acquire new vocabulary easily, their attention spans are short and they need to have language constantly recycled. These stories provide this revision in an exciting way and as such can be used to supplement any main course or form part of a topic-based project.

Why use Photocopiable materials?

- The material is clearly set out and easy to prepare.
- The lessons are well-structured with explicit targets for achievement.
- The emphasis is on direct active teaching.
- The lessons employ a full range of strategies: whole class, group and individual work.

Why use stories for teaching EFL?

- For enjoyment and relaxation: most children enjoy having stories read to them.
- For motivation: stories help children understand by giving language in context and a purpose to learning.
- For consolidation and extension: stories can be chosen to link with the language topic and extend the coursebook activities.
- To provide cross-curricular links, e.g. with Science, Maths, Music, Art, History.
- To recycle and repeat language in a natural way.
- To explore feelings and develop the imagination.
- To focus on the sounds and rhythms of the language in a meaningful way.

Why use traditional and folk tales in the EFL classroom?

- Traditional stories have always provided material for teaching and learning in the mother tongue - they are usually fun and include a strong message with which pupils can identify.
- Children hear stories from an early age in their own culture and by using a tale which is familiar to the child in their mother tongue (e.g. *The Pied Piper*) - they will be able to understand the pattern of events and guess the meaning of unknown language.
- Traditional tales from other countries are culturally interesting - while they may not

already be familiar with some of these (e.g. *The Leopard's Drum*), these tales often have a familiar and simple moral.

How do you choose a story for young learners?

- The story should be short enough to be told in one lesson.
- The story should have a simple and memorable story line.
- The story should contain dialogue.
- The language level of the story should be suitable for the class. It is necessary for 75% of the language to be understood by the class. The remaining 25% of the language will provide exposure to new vocabulary and structures.
- The story should contain repetitive phrases and possibly be linked to a song or rhyme.

Format

The book is split into 6 stories, each containing the Story Text (which is presented in a variety of ways) plus 5 Photocopiable Lessons and 5 pages of accompanying Teachers Notes. Once the teacher has 'told' or played the story, the Photocopiable Pages provide language practise and fun activities for exploiting it.

The stories in this book are: ***The Leopard's Drum***; ***The Old Woman who lived in a Bottle***; ***The Rich Man and the Shoemaker***; ***The Farmer, his Son and the Donkey***; ***The Honey Pot***; and ***The Pied Piper***.

Further information on each of the stories can be found in the Notes on the Stories at the end of this Introduction.

The stories, and the Teacher's Notes which face the corresponding Photocopiable Page are numbered consecutively. Each story follows a language syllabus which is outlined in the Contents pages. The stories have been arranged in order, from fairly simple to more advanced. Consequently, teachers wishing to select a story for the more confident pupils will probably use materials from the second half of the book. However, the Photocopiable Pages are better used in the order given as they build on the language used in the story.

This book is accompanied by a cassette, containing all the stories and listening texts, songs and chants. The cassette is provided as an alternative to the teacher reading the story and it can also be played to provide an example of an English native speaking voice. However, if teachers are confident enough, we recommend that they first tell the stories themselves, and then use the recorded version.

Teacher's notes

The Teacher's Notes contain a list of the vocabulary and structures to be practised and give guidance on preparing and using the Photocopiable Pages. They also include **Warm-up** ideas for pre-teaching difficult vocabulary and optional **Follow-up** activities. These activities will vary in the time they take depending on the ability of the class. Therefore it is left to the teacher's discretion as to whether they have time to do the Follow-up activity or not.

The notes also indicate whether the focus of the **main** activity is for individual, pair, or group work, which skills are practised, and which materials are needed. As there is always flexibility in the approach to teaching younger learners, these activities can be adapted to suit the level of the pupils involved.

Language content

The purpose of these materials is to sometimes teach new language and also to practise or revise vocabulary or structures. The language used in the stories in *Telling Tales* is repeated in various ways and in different contexts throughout the stories. Each story presents new vocabulary which is introduced in the first lesson by the teacher reading the story or playing it from the cassette. As well as this target language, each story also contains some unfamiliar language which is not intended for pupils to learn and repeat. If necessary, explain this language using the mother tongue.

Classroom language

It will be necessary to pre-teach the language used for instructions, if you wish the pupils to use English when they are preparing and doing their activities. Some phrases such as imperatives *stand up /sit down* are covered in the stories. Other phrases which may be useful are: *look at, point to, listen to, cut out, colour in, draw this, pick up, glue this, make a, find a, ask your friend*; plus the classroom items listed in the Materials section: *scissors, crayons, glue, pencils, paper, cassette, puppets*, etc.

Classroom management

Young learners have certain characteristics which have to be considered when planning the use of stories for EFL:

- They tend to be keen and enthusiastic learners, without the inhibitions which older learners sometimes bring to their schooling.
- Young learners need physical movement and activity to help stimulate their thinking.
- They have a short attention span and have very little inhibition.

For the purposes of this book we have assumed class sizes of 16 or more (where pupils can easily work in pairs and groups of about 4 or more). If your classes are larger you may wish to change some of the pair work activities into group activities, and increase your group sizes to 6 or more depending on whether it is a play or a game. If you have smaller classes, then pupils can play some of the group games in pairs or as a class activity (i.e. one large group). For easier classroom management when listening to and reading the story, you could organise your class to sit in a circle on the floor in front of you with the cassette recorder.

Many of the activities require the children to work in pairs. It is a good idea to make the children change partners from time to time.

Photocopiable activities

Activities have been chosen to provide some fun in learning English and to be of interest to children of primary age. While there is a focus on speaking and listening skills there are more reading and writing activities as the stories progress.

The 30 Photocopiable Lessons contain a wide variety of activities including worksheets, board games, card games, sequencing, colour dictation, finger and stick puppets, a survey, a story wheel, story books, drama and things to make and do. Some of the activities require preparation, but as children like cutting, colouring and glueing, try to get them involved as much as possible. It is a useful way to promote co-operation, class participation and to practise classroom language. If the class time is limited, there are activities where the teacher can do the bulk of the preparation to reduce time.

It is useful to ask the pupils to write their names on their worksheets if you intend to keep them. It advisable when pupils are preparing card/board games that they first stick their photocopy onto thin card so that it will last longer. These cards can then be stored for use in another lesson. As well as preparing their own materials to use in class, pupils will also produce a variety of artwork while doing the activities. These can be displayed on the classroom walls or bound together in a story book. These personalised books can then be displayed for open evenings or taken home to show parents.

Games

The stories contain a variety of games – these are valuable activities which help the pupils to understand the vocabulary of the story and the language structures. They all have a language aim and pupils are expected to use as much English as possible while playing them. Games also teach children about the importance of taking turns, following rules, sharing, winning and losing. While the rules of the card games are included in the Teacher's Notes for the specific page, following is a bank of card games which can be used as alternative ideas or as follow ups.

Bingo

Individual

1 Give out the bingo cards with either 12 or 16 blank squares.

2 Each pupil chooses 12 or 16 picture cards and places them face up on the bingo card.

3 The teacher chooses a word and says it out loud.

4 If a pupil has a corresponding picture on his/her bingo card they turn the card face down.

5 The teacher continues with the other words at random.

6 Pupils shout *bingo* when their cards are all face down. Check their answers by asking them to turn their cards and say the words. If they are correct they win the game.

7 Play it again, and ask the pupils to change some of the cards.

Snap

Pairs or in threes

1 Each pair mixes their cards together and puts them into two separate piles.

2 Pupil 1 turns over the first card and says the name of the object/animal and puts it on the table face up.

3 Pupil 2 turns over his/her card and also says the name of the object/animal. Each pupil takes turns turning over the cards from their piles until they get two pictures the same. The first pupil to shout *snap* or place their hand on the card picks up the pile of winning cards.

4 These cards go back at the bottom of the winner's pile. The game continues with this pupil turning over their top card and both pupils taking it in turns to play until one pupil has collected all the cards.

5 If three pupils are involved the game is played in the same way but when one pupil has lost all their cards the remaining two players continue as above.

Memory

Pairs or groups

1 Each pair places the two sets of cards on the table face down and mixes them up.

2 Pupils take it in turns to turn over two cards and say the name of the object/ animal. If they find two the same they keep them. If there are two different pictures, they must replace the cards in the same place on the table.

3 The pupil with the most matching pairs at the end of the game is the winner.

Sequencing

Pairs

1 Pupils play this in pairs. They sit back to back with all their cards on the table in front of them.

2 Pupil 1 arranges his/her cards in an order of their choice and then tells the order to Pupil 2.

3 Pupil 2 has to put his/her cards in the same order.

4 If pupils are familiar with the words, they can say them as quickly as possible to make it more difficult for Pupil 2.

5 Pupils now swap roles and repeat.

4 of a Kind/Happy Families

In groups of 4

1 Pupils use 4 sheets of photocopiable cards and after cutting them out according to the teacher's notes, they mix them up and give them out so that each pupil has the same number of cards. Pupils should hold their cards in their hands without letting the others see them.

2 Tell them that the aim of the game is to collect four pictures which are the same by asking one of the four people for a picture.

3 First each pupil arranges the cards they have already got in sets. If they have four cards of a kind they put them together on the table in front of them and say *I have four ....*

4 Now pupils take turns asking any one in the group by saying *(name) do you have ..., please?* If the pupil asked says *yes* they must hand it over. If they say *no* then the next pupil takes a turn to ask anyone in the group for a picture they want.

5 The game continues until everyone has no cards left. The pupil with the most number of sets is the winner.

Notes on the 6 Stories

The Leopard's Drum

The first story in this book is a West African tale about animals.
A leopard has a superb drum which is wanted by all the other animals, and especially by the Sky God. Of all the animals, it is the smallest and least significant one, the tortoise, that is clever enough to obtain the drum and give it to the Sky God after all the larger and stronger animals have failed.

The story is presented in the form of a three-part shadow puppet play.

The language used focuses on questions such as *Can I have ... ?, Can you lend me ... ?* and *What do you want?* It uses present tense verbs and superlatives.

Cross-curricular links can be made with topics about wild animals, Africa and Art (shadow puppets).

The Old Woman who lived in a Bottle

This story can be used to teach *there is/are*, past tenses *had/was* and rooms/furniture vocabulary. There is a selection of activities to practise all four skills, including ordering pictures from the story, writing dialogue, a wordsearch and a picture dictation. The moral of the story is that people are never content if they always want something bigger and better. The story can be linked to the topics of homes or castles.

The Rich Man and the Shoemaker

This is a traditional story written as a cartoon, which contains the moral that money does not bring happiness. It focuses on the use of prepositions and furniture vocabulary, revision of numbers, ordinals with activities such as bingo and a board game. There is also a survey on bedtime routines, together with reading and writing activities. It fits well with the topics of homes or jobs.

The Farmer, his Son and the Donkey

This is an adaptation of an amusing tale told by La Fontaine. The story pictures a farmer and his son travelling to market on a donkey. On the way they meet many people, all of them offering contradictory advice about who should ride on the donkey and who should walk. Eventually the donkey itself protests about being ridden by anyone. The moral of this story is that it is impossible to please everyone at the same time.

The present continuous tense is used throughout this story, which also emphasises the use of adjectives and comparatives. Lesson activities include writing speech bubbles, games, making a story book, sequencing and drawing pictures in a 'hall of mirrors'. It can be linked to the topics of farm animals and food.

The Honey Pot

This is an adaptation of a traditional story from the Middle East which tells the tale of how the village people get together to plan to give their King a birthday present. They think it is important that everyone contributes to the group present but they are all guilty of trickery.

The language content is more suitable for older primary children as the story contains verbs in the past, present and past continuous tenses.

This story can be linked to the topics of birthdays, animals and food. It also provides an opportunity to act or mime the story using a narrator and six children.

The Pied Piper of Hamelin

This last story is set many years ago in Germany, in a small town which was infested with rats. Activities associated with the story include a chant, picture and word matching, map reading, spot the difference, filling in missing words, memory and making a class frieze.

It uses both the past and present tenses, and gives opportunities for teaching map reading, giving and following directions, and the use of adjectives, prepositions and opposites. The map reading and directional skills can be extended by drawing maps of the local area, and getting the children to give each other directions for going from place to place.

The moral of this story is that it is important to keep promises. It can be linked to the topics of towns, maps and the environment.

The Leopard's Drum

Part 1

Narrator *Leopard is very strong and fierce. He has a big drum and he plays it every day. All the animals want it. The Sky God also wants the drum.*

Sky God Leopard, what a big drum. I want that drum.

Leopard No!

Sky God Can I have your drum, please?

Leopard No!

Sky God Can you lend me your drum, please?

Leopard No!

Sky God Animals of the jungle – bring me that drum and you will get a reward.

Part 2

Narrator *The next day, Python goes to Leopard.*

Leopard What do you want, Python?

Python I want your drum, your big drum.

Leopard Roar.

Python Goodbye, Leopard. *(runs away)*

Narrator *The next day, Elephant goes to Leopard.*

Leopard What do you want, Elephant?

Elephant I want your drum, your big drum.

Leopard Roar.

Elephant Goodbye, Leopard. *(runs away)*

Narrator *The next day, Monkey goes to Leopard.*

Leopard What do you want, Monkey?

Monkey I want your drum, your big …

Leopard Roar.

Monkey Goodbye, Leopard. *(runs away)*

Part 3

Narrator *The next day, Tortoise goes to Leopard. The other animals laugh at her.*

Animals You are small, you can't get the drum.

Leopard What do you want, Tortoise?

Tortoise I want your drum.

Leopard It's a big drum, a huge drum.

Tortoise It's not big. It's tiny.

Leopard Tiny? This is the biggest drum in the jungle!

Tortoise No, the Sky God has got the biggest drum.

Leopard What!

Tortoise It's huge, he can climb inside it.

Leopard Well, I can climb inside my drum. Look at me.

Narrator *Leopard climbs inside his drum, and then Tortoise puts a cooking pot on it. She slowly pushes the drum to the Sky God.*

Tortoise Here is Leopard's drum.

Sky God Well done Tortoise! Let Leopard go, and you can have your reward. What do you want?

Tortoise I want a hard shell so that the other animals cannot hurt me.

Narrator *The Sky God laughs. He gives Tortoise a hard shell and Tortoise is very happy!*

Lesson 1

Language

- *What's this?*
- *Can I have your ... ?*
- *Can you lend me your ... ?*
- animal vocabulary

Materials

- cassette
- Photocopiable pages 10/11 per pupil
- Photocopiable pages 13/15 per group
- small pieces of black card, about 20 cm by 10 cm – one per pupil
- small sticks, about 30 cm long – one per pupil
- scissors, sellotape, crayons
- optional: A screen, which can be made from a thin white sheet of material stretched between two chairs on desks (or held by two pupils) and a lamp, to shine onto the screen from behind (see diagram below).

Warm-up

1 Introduce the story to the children, by telling them that this is a story from West Africa about a leopard who has a huge drum, which all the other jungle animals also want. The story is told as a shadow puppet play and they are going to make their own puppets. The story is divided into three parts.

2 Hold up Photocopiable pages 13 and 15 (if the class cannot see the pages ask them to move to the front of the room). Point to each of the characters in the story in turn and ask *What's this?* Pupils reply *It's a leopard.* Pupils may know the names of the animals but you will have to explain *Sky God.*

3 Explain the differences between *have* and *lend* using classroom objects. For example, *Can I have your pencil?* (pupils gives you their pencil and you keep it): *Can you lend me your book?* (pupils gives you their book, you look at it quickly then give it back). Pupils practise asking each other questions like these in pairs, but answering *no.*

(Teacher's notes continued on page 14.)

Lesson 1

(continued)

Procedure

1 Read or play the cassette for Part 1 of the story.

2 Give out Photocopiable pages 10/11 and divide the class into groups of 3. Get each group to choose a character: narrator, Leopard or Sky God and then read part 1 together.

3 Do the same for Parts 2 and 3 but you will need groups of 5 for re-telling.

4 Now put pupils into groups of 6 and give each group a copy of Photocopiable pages 13 and 15.

5 Each child in the group chooses one of the characters and prepares their puppet as follows:

- Cut roughly round your character.
- Stick it onto a piece of card.
- Cut carefully round its outline.
- Attach the character to the stick using tape.
- Write your name on the back of your shadow puppet.

6 In their groups get them to practise reading the story together (leaving out the narrator's part).

7 Then ask each group to perform their stories in turn using their puppets. The teacher reads the part of the narrator. The pupils can either:

- use the top of a desk or table as the stage while they sit on the floor behind it (as in the diagram below), or
- make shadow puppets and use a screen and lamp (as in the diagram on page 12).

Follow-up

If you have time, or for homework, ask pupils to choose one of the characters in the story. They then draw a picture of it and write 2 or 3 sentences to describe it. Brainstorm some suggestions if necessary e.g. *Leopard - He is strong. He is big. He's got spots.* Pupils could read these out in class and/or display their finished pictures on the walls.

Lesson 2

LISTENING
SPEAKING
READING
WRITING

Language

- story comprehension
- animal vocabulary

Materials

- cassette
- optional: Photocopiable pages 10/11 and shadow puppets
- Photocopiable page 17 per pupil

Warm-up

1 Revise the names of the characters. Hold up a shadow puppet of each character in turn, and ask *Who's this?* Pupils reply, e.g. *It's Monkey.*

2 Play the cassette of the story again. Stop after each part and explain any necessary language, e.g. *fierce, reward, shell.*

3 Ask some simple comprehension questions, for example: *What does 'huge' mean? Does it mean the same as 'big'?* (No, it means 'very big'). *What does Leopard say to Python?* (What do you want?) *Why do the animals run away?* (Because they are afraid of the Leopard). *Why do the animals laugh at Tortoise?* (Because they think she is too small to get the drum from leopard).

4 Optional: Pupils act the story again in groups using their shadow puppets.

Procedure

1 Give a copy of Photocopiable page 17 to each pupil.

2 In the first part they should draw a line matching the animals to the correct speech bubble.

Answers: 1 b 2 d 3 a 4 c

3 Ask the children to read the words in the list next to the crossword. They then find the correct place to write them into the puzzle.

Answers:

		p			m	o	n	k	e	y
		y							l	
		t	o	r	t	o	i	s	e	
		h							p	
l	e	o	p	a	r	d			h	
		n							a	
									n	
									t	

Follow-up

1 Ask the children which other wild animals they think would like to have the Leopard's drum. Use this as an opportunity to introduce the English words for other animals, such as *lion, tiger, giraffe, hyena, zebra, rhinoceros.*

2 Now get each pupil to make up another crossword including some of the new animals. They can include some of the letters as a help or draw picture clues and then swap these with a partner and do each other's.

Match the pictures to the speech bubbles.

1 elephant

2 leopard

3 tortoise

4 Sky God

a It's not big. It's tiny.

b I want your drum, your big drum.

c Can you lend me your drum, please?

d What do you want?

Complete the crossword.

tortoise
leopard
monkey
python
elephant

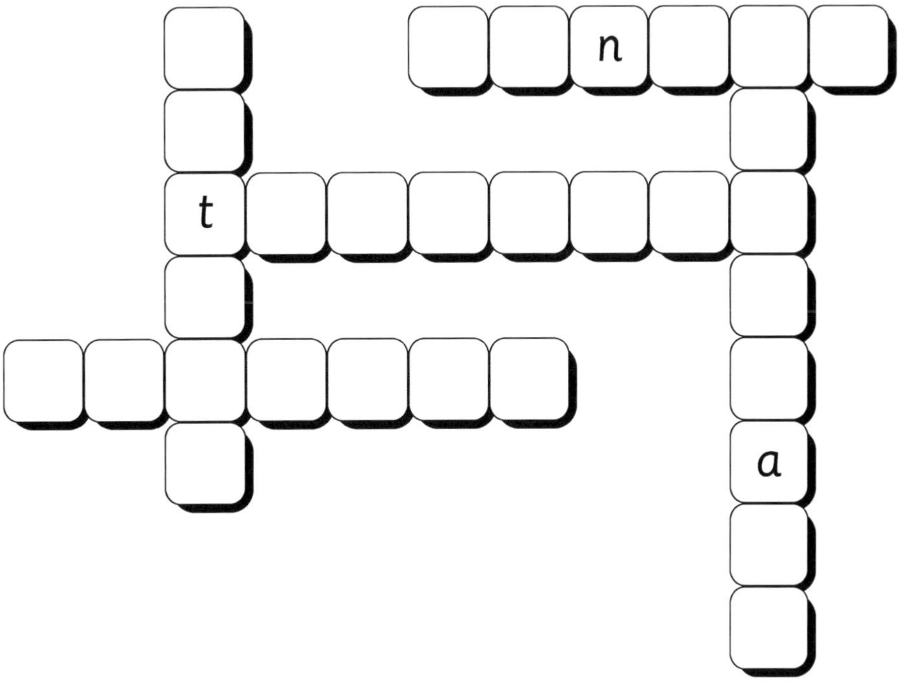

Lesson 3

LISTENING
SPEAKING
READING
WRITING

Language

- adjectives: *big, huge, small, tiny*
- superlatives: *biggest, smallest*

Materials

- Photocopiable page 19 per pupil

Warm-up

If necessary, pre-teach the adjectives using classroom objects:

1 Lay 4 pencils on the desk (one needs to be unusually thin/small and the other larger than a usual sized pencil).

2 Ask one child to put them in order from tiny to huge.

3 Then hold up the small pencil and say, *This is a small pencil. What is it?* Pupils reply. Then repeat with the big/huge/tiny pencils.

4 Now draw/stick some pictures on the board of other objects and say, e.g. *a small book, a huge ball, a tiny rubber.* Pupils come out and point to the correct picture.

Procedure

1 Give a copy of Photocopiable page 19 to each pupil.

2 They complete their worksheets by first writing the correct adjective under the leopard pictures, and then by drawing different sized drums according to the descriptions.

Answers: 1 big 2 tiny 3 huge 4 small

Follow-up

1 Using Photocopiable page 19 ask pupils to tell you which is the *biggest* leopard (number 3) and which is the *smallest* (number 2).

2 Practise these with groups of 3 classroom objects, e.g. *the smallest/biggest rubber.*

3 Play a game where pupils are divided into groups and each group has to find the smallest or biggest book/ruler/rubber/pencil in the classroom.

Write

1

....

2

....

3

....

4

....

Draw

a huge drum

a big drum

a small drum

a tiny drum

Lesson 4

LISTENING
SPEAKING
READING
WRITING

Language

- *Can I have ...?*
- story vocabulary

Materials

- Photocopiable page 21 per pupil
- card, glue, crayons
- cassette

Preparation

1 Give each pupil a copy of Photocopiable page 21. Ask them to colour in the eight pictures.

2 They then glue their page onto a sheet of card and cut along the lines to make eight cards.

Procedure

4 of a kind

1 Divide the class into groups of eight and get them to sit in a circle. Tell them to mix all their cards together.

2 Explain the rules of the game:

- The aim of the game is to collect as many sets of 4 identical cards as possible.
- Choose one person to deal the cards to each person in the circle until they all have eight cards each. Show them how to put these cards into groups of the same kind and keep them in their hand without anyone else seeing their cards.
- The person who is sitting next to the dealer chooses someone in the circle and says *Ana, can I have the leopard please?* If Ana has a leopard she says *Yes, here you are* and gives the card to them, if she doesn't she just says *No, sorry.* The next person in turn chooses someone and asks them for a card they need. When someone has collected 4 pictures of the same animal or object they must put them on the table face down.
- When someone has collected all their sets of cards and has no cards left in their hand they are out.
- The game continues until everyone has no cards left.
- The winner is the person with the most sets of cards on the table.

3 Pupils could also use these cards to play a memory game (see rules on page 5).

Follow-up

Play the song *Can I have your drum, please?* to the pupils. Explain any difficult words. Play it again until the pupils can join in.

Tapescript

Can I have your dr-um, please?
Can I have your dr-um, please?
Can I have your dr-um, please?
No! Please go away!

Python wants your dr-um, please.
Python wants your dr-um, please.
Python wants your dr-um, please.
No! Please go away!

Elephant wants your dr-um, please.
Elephant wants your dr-um, please.
Elephant wants your dr-um, please.
No! Please go away!

Monkey wants your dr-um, please.
Monkey wants your dr-um, please.
Monkey wants your dr-um, please.
No! Please go away!

Tortoise wants your dr-um, please.
Tortoise wants your dr-um, please.
Tortoise wants your dr-um, please.
Look! She's got it now!

Lesson 5

LISTENING
SPEAKING
READING
WRITING

Language

- *Can you lend me ...?*
- classroom items: *pencil, pen, rubber, ruler, book, crayons, chair, table, desk, bag, pencil sharpener, scissors*

Materials

- Photocopiable page 23 per pupil
- crayons
- scissors
- cassette

Warm-up

1. Give out Photocopiable page 23 to each pupil.
2. Point to the objects in the pictures and ask *What's this?* Pupils answer, e.g. *It's a desk.*
3. Play a game: tell the class they have to guess which object you are looking at, e.g. *It is long and thin and you measure with it. (It's a ruler.)*

Procedure

1. Ask the pupils to colour in the 12 objects on the page.
2. Ask them to cut along the lines carefully to make 12 cards. (If possible get them to stick this onto card first.)
3. Divide the class into pairs and tell them they are going to play the game in their pairs A and B.
4. A must ask *Can you lend me something which is ...* e.g. *long and thin.* B replies *Do you want a ...* e.g *pen?*
5. If B guesses correctly they can keep the card. If they guess incorrectly then A must say *I want your ...* and B has to give them the correct card.
6. The winner is the one with the most correct cards at the end.

Follow-ups

I spy

1. Talk about other objects in the classroom e.g. the door, the ceiling, the window, the floor, etc
2. Tell the class they have to guess which object you are looking at when you say *I spy with my little eye something huge/big/small/tiny beginning with ...* Say the first letter of the word and ask the class to say what they think it is.
3. When a pupil guesses correctly they have a turn.

Song

1. Play the animal song again. Get pupils (as a class or in groups) to sing it without the cassette, adding in the names of other animals they know.

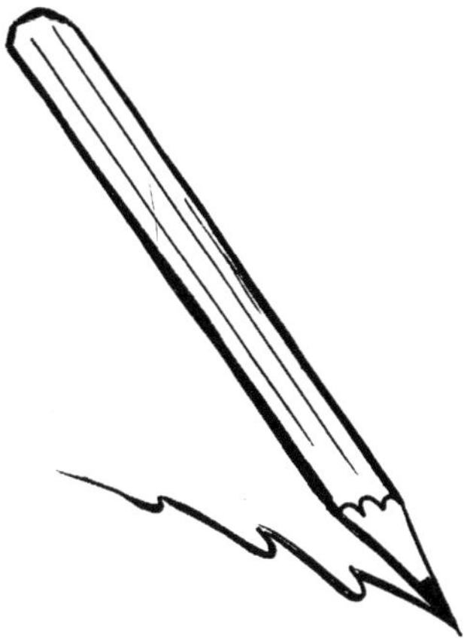
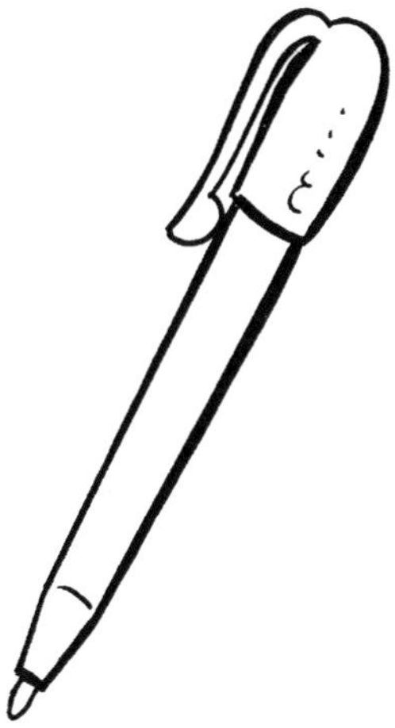
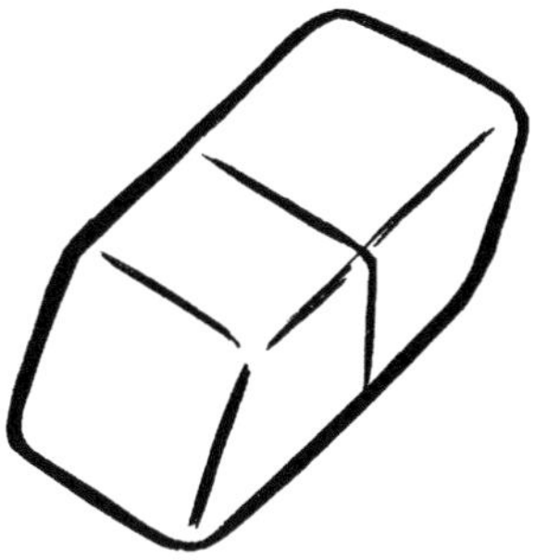
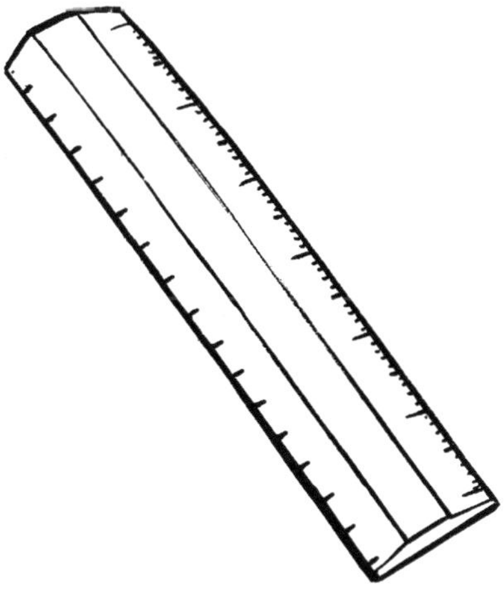

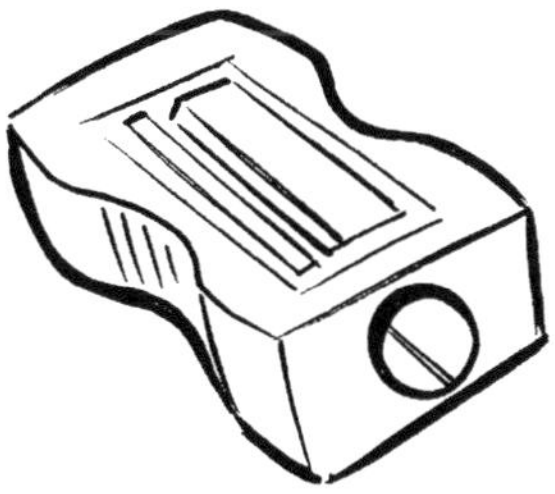

The Old Woman who Lived in a Bottle

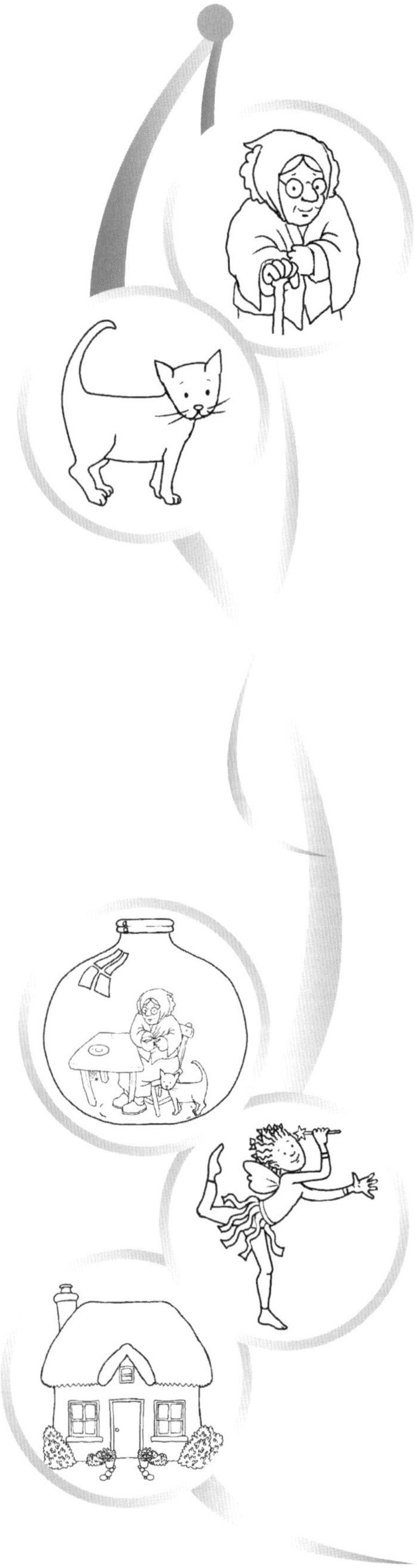

Once there was an old woman who lived in a bottle.
She had a table and a chair and cat.
There was a cup and a saucer on the table.

• • •

One day the old woman was very sad. Her cat was very sad too.

• • •

Just then a fairy came. She had a magic wand.
'What's the matter?' asked the fairy.
'I don't want to live in a bottle,' said the old woman.
'I want to live in a house.'

• • •

The fairy said, 'Stand up, close your eyes, turn around three times and open your eyes.'
So the old woman stood up, closed her eyes, turned around three times and opened her eyes.

• • •

She was in a house. It had a chimney, a roof, two windows and a door. The old woman was very happy. The cat was very happy too.

• • •

But soon the old woman was very sad again.
The fairy came again.
'What's the matter now?' asked the fairy.
'I don't want to live in a house,' said the old woman.
'I want to live in a castle.'

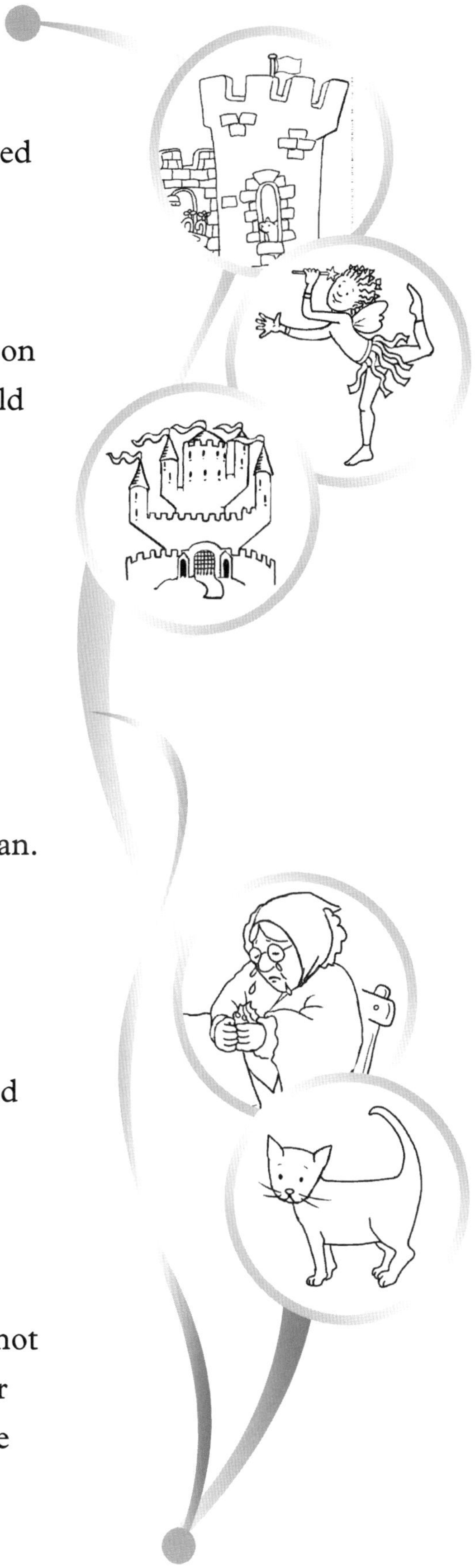

The fairy said, 'Stand up, close your eyes, turn around three times and open your eyes.'
So the old woman stood up, closed her eyes, turned around three times and opened her eyes.

• • •

She was in a castle. It had a big tower with a flag on top. There were many rooms and windows. The old woman and the cat were very happy.

• • •

But soon the old woman was very sad again.

• • •

Suddenly the fairy came again.
'What's the matter now?' asked the fairy.
'I don't want to live in a castle,' said the old woman.
'I want to live in a palace.'

• • •

The fairy said, 'Stand up, close your eyes, turn around three times and open your eyes.' So the old woman stood up, closed her eyes, turned around three times and opened her eyes.

• • •

But the old woman was not in a palace. She was not in a castle. She was not in a house. She was in her bottle again. The old woman was very sad, but the fairy did not come again. Why? Because the old woman was too greedy.

Lesson 1

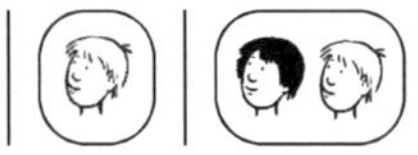

LISTENING
SPEAKING
READING
WRITING

Language

- past tense: *had, was*
- *there is/are*
- *What's the matter?*
- story vocabulary

Materials

- Photocopiable pages 24/25 per pupil
- Photocopiable pages 27 & 29 per pupil
- cassette
- coloured pencils or crayons
- scissors, glue or sellotape

Warm-up

1 Ask the class where they live. Then talk about the kind of house/apartment they live in.

2 Write the words *palace* and *castle* on the board. Ask the class if they would like to live in a palace or a castle. Talk about what it is like inside a palace and a castle.

Procedure

1 Give out copies of the picture story on Photocopiable pages 27 and 29.

2 Look at each picture and ask the class *What can you see in this picture?* This will enable you to pre-teach or revise the important vocabulary e.g. *old woman, fairy, tower.*

3 Read the story out loud while pupils just listen.

4 Play the cassette of the story. Pupils listen and look at the pictures.

5 Play the cassette again. Pause after section 1 and ask pupils to tell you which picture this refers to (second picture on page 27). Point to the number 1 in the box in the corner of the picture. Continue the cassette pausing after each section to allow pupils time to select their pictures. You can do this as a class activity or in pairs to make it easier.

Answers: 5, 1, 9, 6, 2, 11, 3, 12, 7, 10, 4, 8

6 Tell the class that they are going to make a story book from the pictures.

7 They first colour in the pictures, then cut round them on the dotted lines.

8 Show them how to put the pages next to each other in the correct order to make a long line and to sellotape the pictures together on the back. These can then be folded to make a zig-zag book (see diagram below).

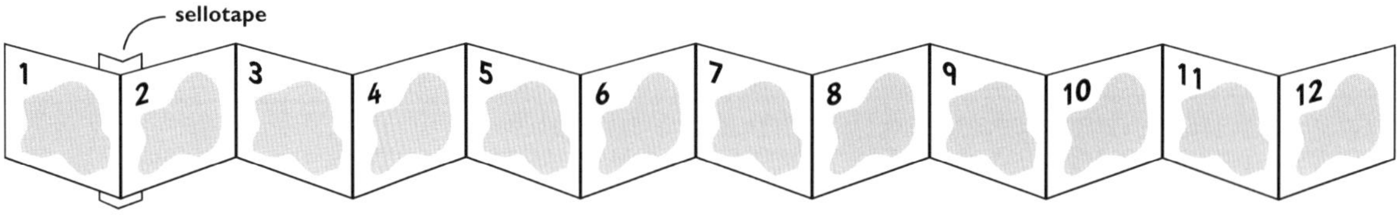

1

Lesson 2

LISTENING
SPEAKING
READING
WRITING

Language

- story vocabulary
- story comprehension

Materials

- cassette
- zig-zag story books they made in the previous lesson
- paper, pencils, scissors

Procedure

1. Play the cassette again. Talk about what the old woman and the fairy say in the story.
2. Divide the class into pairs. Ask them to decide who would like to be the old woman and who would like to be the fairy.
3. Ask the children to work out a short dialogue from the story (it doesn't have to be exactly the same as in the story). They then write their spoken words on a piece of paper and draw a speech bubble around each phrase. Demonstrate this by drawing a speech bubble on the board and writing some words in it.
4. They cut out their speech bubbles and stick them onto the pictures in their story books.
5. They can then practise the dialogue in pairs, and even perform this in front of the class.

Follow-up

In groups of 3, pupils could either:

- make a frieze of the story for the classroom wall, or
- make finger puppets of the old woman, the cat and the fairy, and then act out the story.

Lesson 3

LISTENING
SPEAKING
READING
WRITING

Language

- house and furniture vocabulary: *chimney, roof, windows, door, tower, stairs, living room, kitchen, bedroom, bathroom, table, chair, bed, bath, floor, cup, saucer*

Materials

- Photocopiable page 31 per pupil
- pencils or crayons
- zig-zag story books (made in previous lesson)

Warm-up

1 Talk about the story: ask the class *What happened to the old woman in the bottle?* Give the more fluent children the chance to explain the story. Divide the class into pairs A and B. Ask A to tell the story to B then change over. They can do this in L1 if necessary.

2 Get pupils to open up their zig-zag books. Stick one onto the board. Point to the woman's different homes and ask about rooms and furniture. For example: *What's this? (It's a table.) Is there a kitchen/bathroom/bedroom? (No, there isn't.)*

Procedure

1 Give out copies of Photocopiable page 31 and ask the class to look at the wordsearch.

2 Ask them to read the words above the puzzle with you.

3 Point to the word *windows* which is already circled.

4 Explain that the words go both ways across the puzzle and also up or down or diagonally across the squares.

5 Say *Can you see the word 'table'?*

6 Help pupils who cannot find the word, then tell them to draw a circle around the word.

7 Let pupils find the other words on their own, but go round helping where necessary. (Slower pupils can finish it in their spare time or for homework.)

Answers:

c	u	p	s	a	u	c	e	r
b	h	l	g	h	d	i	j	o
e	w	i	n	d	o	w	s	o
d	c	v	m	k	o	l	b	f
r	h	i	b	n	r	m	a	k
o	a	n	a	b	e	d	t	i
o	i	g	t	n	t	y	h	t
m	r	r	h	p	a	q	r	c
f	l	o	o	r	b	c	o	h
r	s	o	t	u	l	u	o	e
v	w	m	x	y	e	p	m	n

Follow-up

1 Talk about pupil's own homes. Ask, e.g. *How many rooms do you have in your home?*

2 On the board, draw a cross section of a simple house with an open wall showing 4 rooms (2 up and 2 down) with windows and a door.

3 Ask the class to tell you the names of each room. Choose 4 pupils to write the name of each room on the plan on the board. Point to the chimney, roof, windows and door and ask them what they are called and write them on the plan.

4 Ask them if they know any of the names of the furniture and utensils in the house. Get some children to draw the items listed above on the plan and to label them.

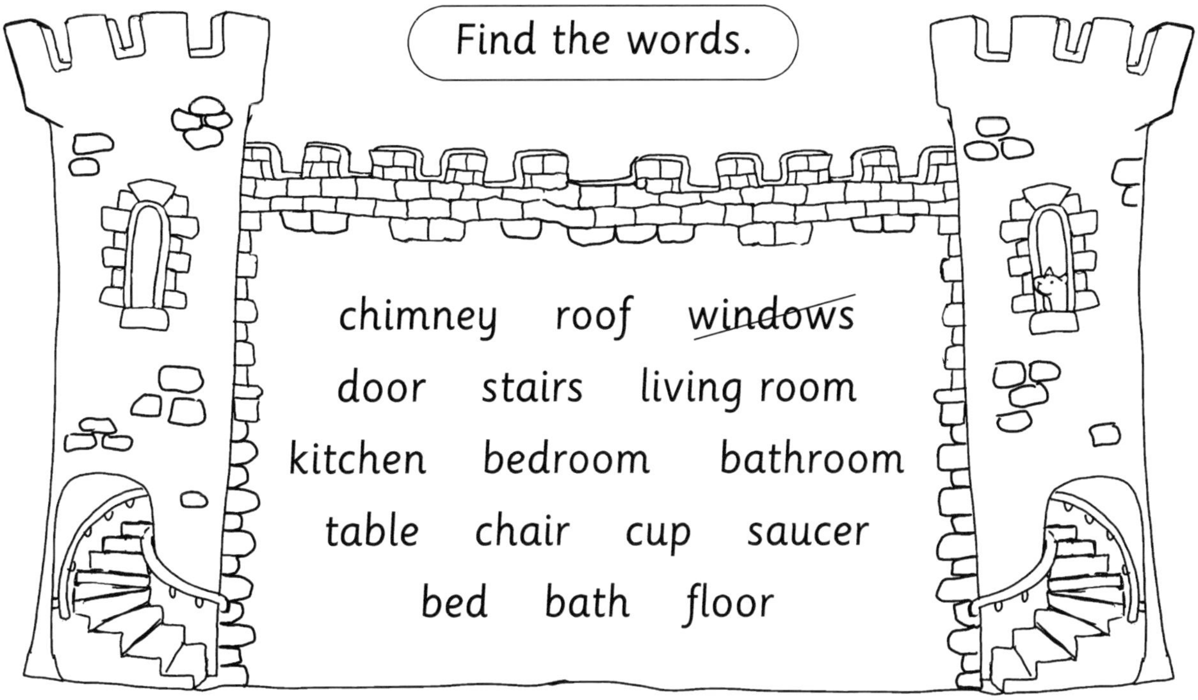

Find the words.

chimney roof ~~windows~~
door stairs living room
kitchen bedroom bathroom
table chair cup saucer
bed bath floor

c	u	p	s	a	u	c	e	r
b	h	l	g	h	d	i	j	o
e	w	i	n	d	o	w	s	o
d	c	v	m	k	o	l	b	f
r	h	i	b	n	r	m	a	k
o	a	n	a	b	e	d	t	i
o	i	g	t	n	t	y	h	t
m	r	r	h	p	a	q	r	c
f	l	o	o	r	b	c	o	h
r	s	o	t	u	l	u	o	e
v	w	m	x	y	e	p	m	n

Lesson 4

LISTENING
SPEAKING
READING
WRITING

Language

- directions: *go up/down the stairs, turn left/right, go straight on, go/climb up/down/through/into/past, open the door*
- castle vocabulary: *ladder, rope, battlements, drawbridge, moat, tower, dungeon, cellar*
- *there is / there are*

Materials

- Photocopiable page 33 per pupil
- cassette
- coloured pencils/pens

Warm-up

1 Read the story to the class again.

2 Explain any difficult words in their own language.

3 Talk about directions, for example how they go out of the classroom to go to the playground or head teacher's room. Say *Which way do you turn?* Put out your right or left hand to show the correct direction. Say *You turn right/left, go straight on, go past the …, go into the …* as appropriate.

Procedure

1 Give out copies of Photocopiable page 33. Ask the class to look at the picture of the castle. Ask *How many rooms can you see in the castle? What are they?* Teach or revise the castle vocabulary listed above.

2 Say *Where is the cat? Can you help him to get out of the castle? Listen to the cassette carefully.* Play the tapescript while pupils listen only.

Tapescript

Draw a line with your pencil.

Can you see the cat? He is in the dungeon.

He goes up the stairs and turns left.

He goes through the cellar and into the kitchen.

Then he climbs up the ladder and turns right.

In the dining room there is a rope.

He climbs up the rope into the bedroom.

He turns right and goes out onto the battlements.

There are two doors. The second is open. He goes through it and down the stairs of the tower.

There is another door at the bottom so he opens this and goes out onto the drawbridge.

He runs over the moat and into the wood.

3 Play the cassette again, pausing after each line. Pupils draw a line following the route described using a coloured pencil.

4 Play it a third time for pupils to check their answers.

Follow-up

1 Tell the class they are going to draw a plan of their own bedroom and put in all the furniture.

2 Do an example on the board first if necessary.

3 When they have finished, ask them to get into pairs and to tell their partner what furniture there is in their home.

Draw the cat's way out of the castle.

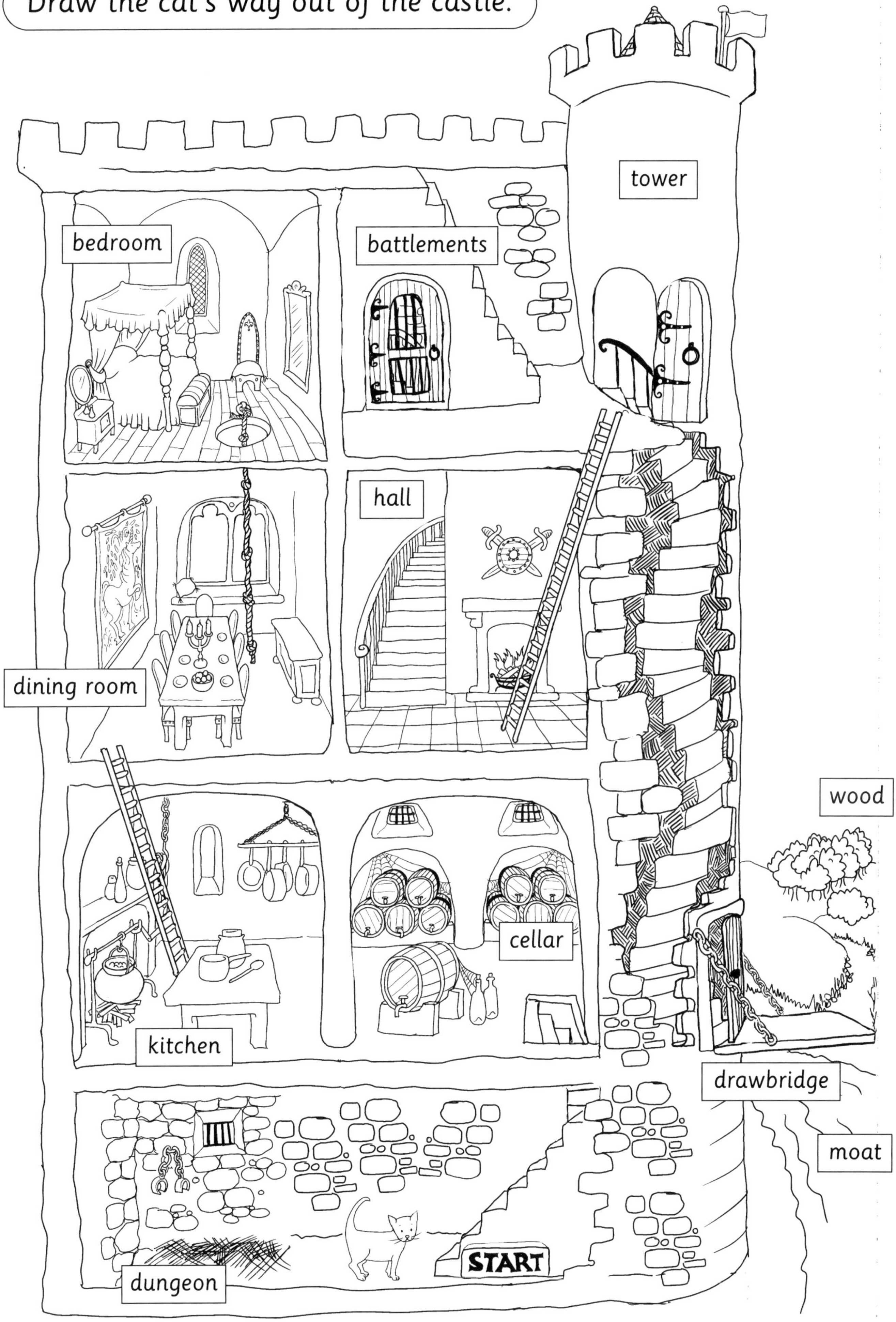

Lesson 5

LISTENING
SPEAKING
READING
WRITING

Language

- *I want/don't want*
- *Where is/where are?*
- rooms/furniture vocabulary

Materials

- Photocopiable page 35 per pair
- glue
- pencils or crayons
- cassette

Warm-up

Talk to the class about where they would live if they could choose anywhere. Ask them if they want to live in a house or an apartment or maybe a palace or a castle. Ask them what they want to put in their dream home.

Procedure

1. Divide the class into pairs. Give each a copy of Photocopiable page 35.

2. Ask pupils if in the story the old woman is happy in her bottle/house/castle. *Where does she really want to live?* (a palace). Tell them they are going to listen to her telling her cat what she wants to put in it.

3. Look at the pictures at the bottom of the page. Ask the class *Where does the cat basket go?* Repeat the question for each item. Tell them to cut each item out carefully.

4. They listen to the cassette again and stick the correct item in the correct room.

Tapescript

Cat: *Where do you want to live old woman?*

Old Woman: *I want a palace with a very big bedroom.*

Cat: *Do you want a kitchen?*

Old Woman: *I want a big kitchen, a big living room and a very big bathroom.*

Cat: *Where do you want to sleep?*

Old Woman: *I want a big bed for myself and a big basket for you in the bedroom.*

Cat: *What do you want in the living room?*

Old Woman: *I want a big fireplace and a big armchair where we can sit when its cold.*

Cat: *What do you want in the kitchen?*

Old Woman: *I want a huge table with lots of food!*

Follow-up

1. Tell the class they are going to draw their own dream home and put in all the rooms and some furniture. This can be a large house/apartment, a castle/palace, or they can design a space-age house with super technological gadgets. Get them to colour and label their drawings.

2. Display these on the walls for others to look at.

The Rich Man and

1

This story is about a shoemaker who lives in a little, old house. He is very poor, but very happy.

2

He makes shoes all day, and he sings while he works.

3

Next door there lives a rich man who counts his money all night. 'I must count my money,' he says. 'One, two, three, four, five, …'

4

In the morning he goes to bed. But he can't sleep because the shoemaker sings all day. So, he goes to see the shoemaker.

5

'Please stop singing. I can't sleep. Here is a bag of money if you stop'. 'Thank you,' says the shoemaker.

6

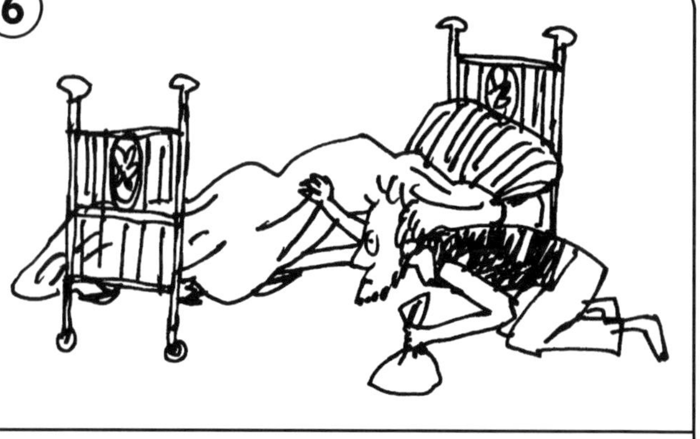

The shoemaker worries about the money all night. 'I must hide it under the bed,' he says.
He goes to bed, but he can't sleep.

the Shoemaker

7

'I must hide the money on the cupboard,' he says.
He goes to bed, but he can't sleep.

8

'I must hide the money in the fridge,' he says.
He goes to bed, but he can't sleep.

9

'I must hide the money behind the chair,' he says.
He goes to bed but he can't sleep.

10

The shoemaker is very unhappy. He stops singing. He stops making shoes. He can't sleep.

11

'I must give the money back to the rich man,' he says.

12

The shoemaker is poor again. He makes shoes all day and he sings while he works. But … he is very happy!

The Rich Man and the Shoemaker

Lesson 1

LISTENING
SPEAKING
READING
WRITING

Language

- story vocabulary: *house, money, shoemaker, rich man, rich, old, poor, happy,* etc
- present tense questions: *What can you see...? Does the ...? Do the...? Is the?*
- present tense verbs: *live, sing, sleep, work, eat*

Materials

- a copy of Photocopiable pages 36/37 per pupil
- a copy of Photocopiable page 39 per pupil
- cassette

Warm-up

Ask the class questions about where they buy their shoes. Tell them this is a story about a happy shoemaker and a rich man.

Procedure

1 Give out copies of the cartoon story on pages 36/37. Look at each picture and ask the class, *What can you see in picture one?* etc.

2 Play the cassette and point to the pictures at the same time.

3 Then ask the pupils some simple comprehension questions: *Is the shoemaker happy? Where does he live?*

4 Ask the pupils to turn their stories over so that they cannot read them. Give out copies of the worksheet on page 39. Pupils do part A by reading the questions and circling the correct answer.

Answers: 1 No 2 No 3 Yes 4 No 5 No 6 No 7 Yes 8 Yes

5 Ask them to do part B by reading the instructions and drawing the story items from memory. They can swap worksheets and compare each other's pictures.

Follow-up

1 Play/read the story again.

2 Tell pupils they are going to play a game called 'Chinese Whispers'.

3 Ask them to sit in a circle and get one pupil to whisper a short sentence from the story to the pupil on their left. This pupil then whispers it to the pupil next to them, and so on.

4 Ask the last pupil to repeat the sentence.

Part A

1	Does the shoemaker live in a new house?	Yes / No
2	Is the shoemaker rich?	Yes / No
3	Does he sing while he works?	Yes / No
4	Does the rich man count his money all day?	Yes / No
5	Does the rich man sleep at night?	Yes / No
6	Does the shoemaker hide the money behind the cupboard?	Yes / No
7	Does the shoemaker give the money back to the rich man?	Yes / No
8	Is the shoemaker happy again?	Yes / No

Part B

Draw an old house.

Draw the shoemaker.

Draw a bag of money.

Draw the rich man.

Draw the cupboard.

Lesson 2

LISTENING
SPEAKING
READING
WRITING

Language

- story vocabulary: *shoemaker, money, cupboard, fridge, shoes, bed, morning, night, house, rich man, chair, shop*

Materials

- a copy of the story on Photocopiable pages 36/37 per pair
- cassette
- a copy of Photocopiable page 41 per pupil
- scissors
- crayons (optional)

Warm-up

Revise story vocabulary by giving out copies of the story and saying, *Point to the money. Point to the rich man. Point to the cupboard.* Pupils point to each item in their pairs. To make it more fun, the pupil who points to the correct item first in each pair gets a point. At the end ask *Who got 6 points? Who got 3?*

Procedure

1. Give out copies of Photocopiable page 41. Tell pupils they are going to play a game called Bingo.
2. Ask them to cut out the 12 picture cards carefully. Then cut round their bingo card.
3. Each child chooses 9 cards and places them face up on the bingo card.
4. Choose one word and say it out loud. If a pupil has the corresponding picture he/she turns the card face down.
5. Continue with the other words.
6. Pupils shout *bingo* when their 9 cards are face down. Check their answers by getting them to turn over their cards and say the words. If they are correct they win the game.
7. Ask pupils to choose another 9 cards and play it again.

Follow-up

1. Read/play the story to the children again. Ask more complicated questions: *Where does the shoemaker live?* (in a little old house) *Who lives next door?* (the rich man) *Who lives next door to you? Why can't the rich man sleep in the daytime?* (because the shoemaker sings all day) *Are there are times when you can't sleep at night?* (possible answers include *because it's too noisy, because I am sad*).
2. Ask pupils to draw a picture of the rich man at night or of the shoemaker during the day. Then ask the children to say something about their picture, e.g. *The rich man can't sleep at night. The shoemaker sings all day.*

1000
Shop

Lesson 3

LISTENING
SPEAKING
READING
WRITING

Language

- story vocabulary
- prepositions: *in, on, under, behind, next to, between*
- *Where is the ...?*
- *first, second, third, fourth*

Materials

- a copy of Photocopiable page 43 per pupil
- cassette

Warm-up

1 Revise the prepositions which appear in the story (*in, on, under, behind*) using classroom objects. For example: *Where is the book?*

2 Teach the new prepositions (*next to, between*) in the same way. For example place a rubber between two books and say
The rubber is between the books. Where is the rubber?

Procedure

1 Ask the class these questions:

In the story, where does the shoemaker hide the money the first time?
Where does he hide it the second time?
Where does he hide it the third time?
Where does he hide it the fourth time?

2 Give out copies of Photocopiable page 43.

3 Play the listening text on the cassette. Pause after each number to give pupils time to draw the money in the correct place.

4 If necessary, play the listening text again straight through for pupils to check their answers.

Tapescript

The money is on the bed.

The money is in the cupboard.

The money is next to the fridge.

The money is under the chair.

The money is behind the shoes.

The money is between the shop and the house.

Follow-up

Tell the class they are going to play Hide and Seek. Ask them to close their eyes and hide a rubber in the classroom. Tell them to open their eyes and then ask, *Is it on ...? Is it under...? Is it in ...?* The child who guesses where the rubber is gets to hide it next time. You can also play this as a team game with half the class hiding an object and the other half asking questions.

1

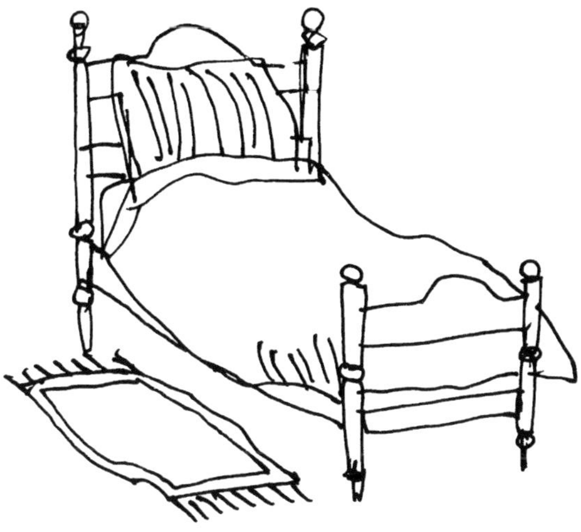

2

3

4

5

6

Lesson 4

LISTENING
SPEAKING
READING
WRITING

Language

- present simple verbs: *sing, count, hide, spell*
- numbers 1-40

Materials

- a copy of Photocopiable page 45 per pair
- a dice per pair
- a counter for each pupil

Warm-up

Ask the children to look at the boardgame on Photocopiable page 45. Count the numbers1-40 out loud. They can also colour in the board if they wish.

Procedure

1 Divide the class into pairs.

2 Read the words on the board with the class. Explain the rules of the game:
   - Each player throws the dice. The player with the highest number goes first.
   - Players take it in turn to throw the dice and move around the board (counting in English as they do so)
   - When they land on a square with a question they have to read it and answer it. If they can't answer it they go back to where they were before.
   - When they land on a square with the shoemaker or the rich man's face, they follow the instructions on it.
   - The winner is the first player to reach the bag of money in the centre.

Follow-up

Play a version of 'Simon Says' but say *The Shoemaker Says … stand up sit down, stand next to, put the book on/in/under, touch …* etc.

START
1
2
3 Can you sing a song?
4
5 Go back to square 2.
6
7 Can you spell 'shoemaker'?
8 Go forward 5 squares.
9
10 Go back to square 6.
11 Where does the shoemaker hide the money the first time?
12
13
14 Go forward 4 squares.
15
16 Go back to square 12.
17
18
19 Where does he hide the gold the second time?
20
21
22 Go forward 3 squares.
23
24 Where does he hide the gold the third time?
25
26 Go back to square 15.
27
28 Go back to square 23.
29
30 Where does he hide the gold the fourth time?
31
32 Go forward 5 squares.
33 Why does he give the money back?
34 Go back to square 27.
35
36 Go back to square 31.
37
38 Can you count up to 40?
39
40
41 FINISH

Lesson 5

LISTENING
SPEAKING
READING
WRITING

Language

- bedtime activities: *have a shower/bath, brush my teeth, comb my hair, feed my pets, get my schoolbag ready, read a book*
- *must*

Materials

- a copy of Photocopiable page 47 per pupil
- cassette

Warm-up

1 Talk about what the shoemaker must do before he goes to bed.

2 Talk to the class about what they must do before they go to bed.

Procedure

1 Give out copies of Photocopiable page 47, then divide the class into groups of 5 or 6 pupils. Look at the list of bedtime activities with the class.

2 Tell each pupil in each group to choose different pupils to ask questions for the survey. Try to arrange it so that each group asks everyone in the class. Tell them to ask *Must you have a shower? Must you clean your teeth?* etc.

3 If a pupil answers *Yes* they must put a tick in the chart; if they answer *No* they put a cross.

4 When they have finished they go back into their groups to collate their information. They write the total number of ticks in the 'Total' column, then each pupil adds their totals together to get a 'Group total' which they write in the final column in the chart.

5 The pupils can then present their information, e.g. as a bar chart, collage, graph or pie chart (see diagrams).

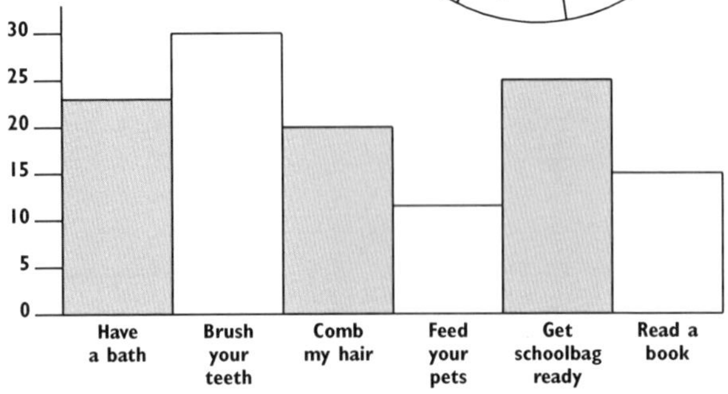

Follow-up

1 Play the song *This is the way ...* on the cassette. Get pupils to mime the actions as they listen.

2 Play the song again and get the class to join in, singing and doing the actions.

3 Split the class into 6 groups, and get each group to make up a verse for a new song *This is the way I ... before I go to school / at my birthday party / on a Sunday morning,* etc.

Tapescript

1. *This is the way I have a bath,*
   have a bath, have a bath,
   This the way I have a bath,
   before I go to bed.
2. *This is the way I brush my teeth ...*
3. *This is the way I comb my hair ...*
4. *This is the way I feed my pets ...*
5. *This is the way I get my bag ready ...*
6. *This is the way I read a book ...*

What must you do at bedtime?

	✔ or ✘	Total	Group total
 Have a shower/bath			
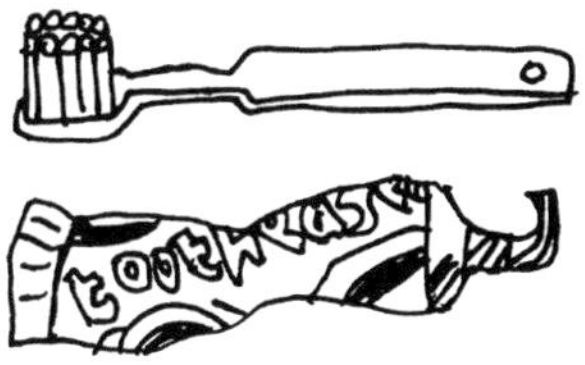 Brush your teeth			
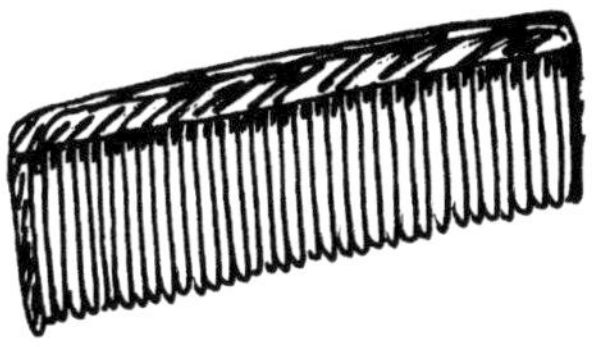 Comb my hair			
 Feed your pets			
 Get schoolbag ready			
 Read a book			

The Farmer, his Son and the Donkey

It is a hot, sunny day. A farmer is going to market on his donkey. His son is walking behind him. They want to buy ten eggs, a whole cheese, and a loaf of bread.

Soon they meet a man. He is sitting under a tree playing his flute.

Flute player: *Where are you going?*

Farmer: *We are going to the market.*

Flute player: *Oh dear! Why are you riding the donkey while your son is walking? You are bigger and stronger than him. He must ride the donkey.*

So, they change places. Now the son is riding the donkey and the farmer is walking.

Soon they meet a builder. He is carrying some bricks.

Builder: *Where are you going?*

Farmer: *We are going to the market.*

Builder: *Oh dear! Why are you riding the donkey while your father is walking? You are younger than him. He must ride the donkey too.*

So the farmer gets on the donkey too. Now they are both riding along the road.

Soon they meet an old man. He is walking his dog.

Old man: *Where are you going?*

Farmer: *We are going to the market.*

Old man: *Oh dear! Why are you both riding the donkey? You are heavy and the donkey is sad.*

So the farmer and his son get off the donkey. Now they are all walking along the road.

Soon they meet a tourist who is buying a postcard. He is laughing and laughing.

Tourist: *Where are you going?*

Farmer: *We are going to the market.*

Tourist: *Oh dear! Why are you all walking? The donkey is tired.*

So the farmer and his son pick up the donkey. Now they are carrying him.

But the donkey kicks and kicks until he is free. The farmer and his son land in a puddle!

Lesson 1

LISTENING
SPEAKING
READING
WRITING

Language

- questions: *What can you see? What is he/are they doing?*
- present continuous: *sitting, walking, riding, playing, going, carrying*
- present simple
- story vocabulary: *farmer, son, donkey, flute, builder, man, tourist*

Materials

- a copy of Photocopiable pages 48/49 per pair
- cassette
- a copy of Photocopiable page 51 per pair
- scissors
- crayons (optional)

Warm-up

Tell the children you are going to read a funny story about a farmer, his son and their donkey. They are on their way to market. Ask the children if they ever go to a market in their town. *What do they buy there? How do they go there? By car/bus/on foot?*

Procedure

1 Give out copies of the story on Photocopiable pages 48/49, one between two will do.

2 Look at each picture and ask the class *What can you see in this picture?*

Possible answers: *a man, a man under a tree, a man playing a flute, a boy riding a donkey, a man and a boy in the water*, etc.

3 Read the story to the class. As you do so point to each picture and get the pupils to also point to each picture on their copies as it is being talked about.

4 Play the cassette, and pause after each character speaks. Ask the children to repeat what the character says (you can do this phrase by phrase).

5 After they have listened to the whole tape, ask the children the following questions: *What does the old man/builder/tourist say to the farmer?*

6 Divide the children into groups of six. Give each child in each group a character to play (farmer, son, flute player, builder, old man, tourist). Ask the children to practise saying the words spoken by their character. The children playing the farmer and his son can speak together.

Follow-up

1 Give out Photocopiable page 51 and read through the word cards with the class.

2 Ask pupils to cut out their cards carefully. Then they match the words to the pictures in pairs. Check their answers.

3 Now tell pupils they are going to play a game called 'Snap'.

4 Each pair places their word cards together in a pile face down (pile A) and then their picture cards together (pile B).

5 Pupil one turns over the first card from pile A and reads it out loud.

6 Pupils take turns turning over the cards from pile B until they get the picture that corresponds with the word card. Then the first pupil to shout *snap* scores a point.

7 These cards go back in the piles and pupil 2 turns over a word card. The winner is the pupil with the most points at the end of the game.

farmer

donkey

builder

tourist

son

old man

dog

flute player

Lesson 2

LISTENING
SPEAKING
READING
WRITING

Language

- present continuous tense: *sitting, playing, carrying, walking, riding, buying, laughing, going*
- *What is he doing? What are they doing?*
- story vocabulary

Materials

- cassette
- a copy of Photocopiable pages 48/49 per pair
- a copy of Photocopiable page 53 per pupil
- scissors

Warm-up

Ask the children comprehension questions about the story, for example: *Where are the farmer and his son going? Who do they meet on the way? What do they do?*

Procedure

1 Play the cassette, and ask the children to listen to the story again.

2 Give out one copy of Photocopiable pages 48/49 between two.

3 Then ask them to look at the first picture. Ask yes/no questions: *Is he standing under the tree? Is he playing a guitar?* etc. Then ask *What is the man doing? (He is sitting under a tree. He is playing his flute)*. Proceed like this with the other pictures.

4 Give out copies of Photocopiable page 53. Ask individual children to read out the sentences under the pictures.

5 Then pupils complete the activity by writing the number of the corresponding picture in the box next to each sentence.

Answers: 1 f 2 g 3 a 4 c 5 b 6 e 7 h 8 d

6 Tell pupils they are now going to play a card game called Sequencing. First they cut out the 8 picture cards at the top of page 53 and play according to the rules below:

- They get into pairs and sit back to back with all their cards in front of them.
- Pupil 1 arranges his/her cards in any order and then tells the order to pupil 2, by describing what is on the card. For example, *the tourist is buying a postcard, the boy is riding the donkey …*
- Pupil 2 has to put his/her cards in the same order.
- Pupil 2 can check if he/she is correct by looking at pupil 1's cards, or by reading out the letters on the card in order.
- Pupils now change roles and repeat.

Follow-up

The class can play a miming game. Ask them to come out individually and perform a mime in front of the class (e.g. *washing hands, writing a letter*). Ask the children *What is he/she doing?* They should answer by describing the action, the pupil who gets it correct has a turn to mime.

1	The builder is carrying some bricks.	☐
2	The tourist is laughing.	☐
3	The old man is walking his dog.	☐
4	The man is sitting under a tree.	☐
5	The tourist is buying a postcard.	☐
6	The man is playing a flute.	☐
7	The farmer is going to the market.	☐
8	The farmer and his son are riding the donkey.	☐

Lesson 3

LISTENING
SPEAKING
READING
WRITING

Language

- present continuous tense: *he/she is, they are + going, carrying, walking, playing, sitting, riding, running, buying, laughing,* etc

Materials

- a copy of Photocopiable page 55 per pupil

Warm-up

Introduce other present continuous verbs using pictures or drawings on the board, e.g. *Is she playing football? No, she's playing the guitar. Is he sitting under a tree? No, he's sitting on a chair.*

Procedure

1 Give out copies of Photocopiable page 55.

2 Ask pupils to look at the two pictures A and B and to find 8 differences (they circle the difference in picture B). Pupils compare their answers in pairs.

3 Now pupils correct the sentences underneath.

Answers:
1. She is riding a horse.
2. He is walking his dog.
3. They are buying ice creams.
4. It is walking.
5. They are playing football.
6. It is sitting in the tree.
7. He is carrying an umbrella.
8. They are laughing.

Follow-up

Pupils can play a team mime game:

- Write 10 different actions on 10 pieces of paper.
- Split the class into 2 teams.
- The first 2 players from each team come to the front of the class. Show them the first action.
- They each mime the action to their team who try to guess it by asking yes/no questions: *Are you walking your dog?*
- The first team to guess it correctly gets a point.
- The 2nd players from each team now come out and mime the 2nd action.

In picture A …	**In picture B …**
The woman is riding a bike.	She is ....
The man is running.	He is ....
The boys are buying sweets.	They are ....
The dog is sleeping.	It is ....
The girls are playing tennis.	....
The cat is sitting under a tree.	....
The man is carrying a bag.	....
The girls are crying.	....

Lesson 4

LISTENING
SPEAKING
READING
WRITING

Language

- adjectives: *sad, happy, heavy, young, strong, big*

Materials

- a copy of Photocopiable page 57 per pupil
- scissors
- crayons/coloured pencils
- stapler
- cassette

Warm-up

Look at the story again. Point to the different characters and ask questions: *Is he strong/heavy/happy?* Then say a character and pupils have to describe them, e.g. *He is young.*

Procedure

1 Give out copies of Photocopiable page 57. Tell pupils they are going to make their own story books about the donkey.

2 First they should colour in the pictures.

3 Then they read the speech bubbles at the bottom, cut them out and stick them on to the corresponding picture.

4 They have to make up their own ending to the story by drawing a picture in empty frame 5 and writing their own speech bubble for the donkey.

5 Finally, they cut out the six pictures and lay them one on top of the other (with 1 at the top). Then they staple the pages together at the left hand side to make a book.

Follow-up

Play the rhyme to the class. Explain any words they don't know. Get the pupils to join in with the cassette, then they could sing the rhyme in groups.

Tapescript

If I had a donkey that would not go
Would I beat him? Oh, no, no, no!
I'd put him in the barn and give him some corn
The best little donkey that ever was born

6

He is heavy.

He is young.

I am sad.

I am happy now!

They are strong.

Lesson 5

LISTENING
SPEAKING
READING
WRITING

Language

- comparatives of adjectives: *big /bigger, strong/stronger, young/younger, heavy/heavier, sad/sadder*

Materials

- a copy of Photocopiable page 59 per pupil
- coloured pencils
- poster-sized sheet of paper per group
- one A4 sheet of paper per pupil
- cassette

Warm-up

1 Ask the class if they have ever seen a hall of mirrors at the fair. If so ask them what happened when they looked at themselves in the mirrors. Discuss how the mirrors change what they look like (the mirrors are not like a normal mirror, they distort and make you look different).

2 Discuss how you can look *bigger, stronger, younger, heavier, sadder*. Mime these adjectives and ask the children to copy you.

Procedure

1 Give out Photocopiable page 59.

2 Tell the class to imagine that the farmer, his son, the donkey, the man and the builder went to the fair on the way to the market. At the fair they went to see the hall of mirrors.

3 Ask the class to look at the pictures on the left side of the page which show what they all normally look like.

4 Play the cassette for the listening text while pupils listen only.

Tapescript

1 The old man is stronger.

2 The farmer is sadder.

3 The son is younger.

4 The builder is bigger.

5 The donkey is heavier.

5 Then play it again stopping after each section to give pupils time to draw what the characters look like in the right side of the mirror.

Follow-up

1 Ask the children to get into groups of five/six.

2 Tell them to choose one of the characters from the story.

3 Ask them to draw their character on the sheet of paper, colour and cut it out.

4 They then each stick their characters onto the poster and write a caption below each using the structure: *The farmer is stronger than the old man; the son is younger than the builder, the donkey is sadder than the dog*, etc.

5 They can display their collage posters on the board for other groups to see.

6 Finish by singing the rhyme from Lesson 4 again.

The Honey Pot

Narrator: *A long time ago, a king lived in a small village. It was his birthday. The villagers wanted to give him a present.*

Villagers: What can we give the King for his birthday?

Narrator: *One man said…*

Man: I know! Let's give him some bread.

Narrator: *They all shook their heads and said …*

Villagers: No, the King has a baker who bakes the best bread in the land.

Narrator: *One woman said …*

Woman: I know! Let's give him some milk and cheese.

Narrator: *They all shook their heads and said …*

Villagers: No, the King has a goat which gives him the best milk and cheese in the land.

Narrator: *A little girl called Nora said …*

Nora: I know! Let's give him some honey.

Villagers: Honey, why honey?

Nora: Well, the king loves honey. If we all give one cup of honey we can fill a large pot and it will last for many years.

Narrator: *The villagers smiled and nodded. They went home to get their cups of honey. Nora opened her kitchen cupboard and took out a cup and her little pot of honey. Nora loved honey, so she did not want to give any to the king. She had an idea. She put her honey pot back in the cupboard and filled her cup with water. She said …*

Nora: The king can't taste one cup of water in the pot with all the honey!

Narrator: *So, she took her cup and waited with the villagers. She watched as everyone emptied their cup into the large pot. Nora emptied her cup into the pot too. Then the villagers asked the King to come to the village to get his birthday present. The king arrived. He looked at the pot in front of him. The people shouted …*

Villagers: It's honey! Try it.

Narrator: *The King put his finger in the pot and tasted it. He looked at the villagers and said …*

King: Is this a joke?

Narrator: *The villagers shook their heads. The king shouted …*

King: This pot is full of water!

Narrator: *Everyone stared at the king and said …*

Villagers: What has happened?

Narrator: *Can you guess? Everyone in the village had the same idea as Nora. They all kept their honey and filled their cup with water instead.*

Lesson 1

LISTENING
SPEAKING
READING
WRITING

Language

- story vocabulary
- past tenses
- *Which is sentence number ...?*
- numbers 1-12

Materials

- a copy of Photocopiable pages 60/61 per pupil
- cassette
- a copy of Photocopiable page 63 per pupil
- scissors, glue

Warm-up

Ask the class if they have tried honey before? Do they like it? Where does honey come from? Would they like a pot of honey for their birthday present? (Do this in L1 if necessary.) Tell them they are going to hear a story about a birthday and a pot of honey.

Procedure

1 Write the following questions on the board:
Whose birthday is it?
Where does he live?
What is the girl's name?
What do the villagers decide to give him for a birthday present?
What do the villagers give him in the end?

2 Play the cassette for the story and ask pupils to listen for the answers to the questions. They can discuss their answers in pairs.

Answers:
the king's / in a village / Nora / a pot of honey / a pot of water

3 Give out copies of Photocopiable pages 60/61. Read through the story again. Note: this story contains some language pupils may not know so use mime as much as possible to explain actions, and point to items/pictures of any difficult vcocabulary as you are telling the story.

4 Let pupils to ask if there are any words they really don't understand, e.g. *What does 'taste' mean?*

5 Give out copies of Photocopiable page 63. Explain that these are the sentences people speak in the story but they are in the wrong order. Read through each sentence with the class.

6 Ask pupils to cut around the dotted lines carefully and to arrange the sentences in the correct order on their desks. (If you prefer you can just ask pupils to number the sentences in order.) If necessary, play the cassette for the story while they do this.

7 Get individual pupils to read out the sentences to check their order.

Answers:
h, k, a, j, e, c, l, g, b, i, d, f.

8 The pupils can now stick the sentences onto a sheet of paper or into their notebooks in the correct order.

Follow-up

1 Tell the class that they are going to mime and act out the story.

2 Put them in groups of 6 or more. Choose a narrator and the main characters: Nora, the king, a man and a woman, the others read the part of the villagers together.

3 Give them time to practise, encourage them to mime the actions as far as they can. Ask them to come to the front of the class to act it out.

a No, the King has a baker who bakes the best bread in the land.

b The king can't see one cup of water in the pot with all the honey!

c I know! Let's give him some honey.

d Is this a joke?

e No, the King has a goat which gives him the best milk and cheese in the land.

f This pot is full of water!

g Well, the king loves honey. If we all give one cup of honey we can fill a large pot and it will last for many years.

h What can we give the King for his birthday?

i It's honey! Try it.

j I know! Let's give him some milk and cheese.

k I know! Let's give him some bread.

l Honey, why honey?

Lesson 2

LISTENING
SPEAKING
READING
WRITING

Language

- food vocabulary: *honey, bread, cheese, milk, etc*
- *What do you like? Do you like …?*

Materials

- a copy of Photocopiable page 65 per pupil
- cassette with story and chant
- coloured pencils or crayons

Warm-up

Play the story on the cassette again. Talk about what the King and the villagers eat for breakfast. Ask pupils: *What do you like for breakfast?*

Procedure

1 Give out the copies of Photocopiable page 65 then divide the class into groups of 5 or 6 pupils. Look at the list and read the names of the foods with the class.

2 Tell each group to choose 5 pupils to ask questions for the survey. Tell them to ask *Do you like honey/milk/bread/cheese for breakfast?* If a pupil answers *yes*, they put a tick in the first column, if they answer *no* they put a cross. They should also ask *What do you like for breakfast?* and then write the name of any other food mentioned in the blank space. When they have finished they write the total number of ticks in the right hand column of the chart.

3 Tell the class to go back to their groups and to add their totals together and to write these in the relevant boxes below the chart. In the two empty boxes they should write the name of the 2 other most popular choices plus their totals.

4 Ask the class *Which food do you like the most? Which one do you like the least?*

Follow-up

1 Write the words of the chant on the board and read the words with the class.

2 Say the words of the chant together with the class.

3 Play the cassette of the chant.

4 Ask them to clap their hands as they say the words.

5 Ask them to stand up and repeat the words and do the actions as they say the chant.

Chant tapescript

I like honey, I like cheese.

I can jump and touch my knees.

I like honey, I like bread

I can jump and touch my head.

What do you like for breakfast?

	✔ or ✘	Total
honey		
milk		
bread		
cheese		
other		

Class totals

Lesson 3

LISTENING
SPEAKING
READING
WRITING

Language

- story vocabulary
- present tense verbs: *give, has/have, love, fill, put, try, know*

Materials

- a copy of the story on Photocopiable pages 60/61 per group
- a copy of Photocopiable page 67 per group
- cassette
- coloured pencils/ crayons
- scissors
- split paper fasteners

Warm-up

Talk about birthdays. Ask the children when their birthday is. Ask what they got for their birthday present. What do they want for their next birthday?

Procedure

1 Put the class into groups and give each group a copy of Photocopiable pages 60/61 and page 67.

2 Play the cassette of the story again. Stop the cassette at any difficult point and ask *What is he saying? What does he/she do?*

3 Ask the pupils to colour in the pictures on their story wheel. Show them how to cut out the two circles, and to cut out the wedge in circle A. Place circle A on top of circle B and make a hole in the centre. Put the split paper fastener through the middle of the two circles to join them. They can turn the top circle to see the story.

4 Read the story again and tell them to turn their wheel to see the pictures, as they come to each part.

5 Ask the pupils to work together in their groups to move the story wheel. As they reach each picture they say a sentence that corresponds using direct speech, for example:

1. It's the king's birthday.
2. Let's give him some bread.
3. Let's give him some milk and cheese.
4. Let's give him some honey.
5. I don't want to give honey to the king.
6. The king can't taste one cup of water.
7. It's honey. Try it.
8. Is this a joke?

6 Alternative: to make this more difficult, the pupils can use the story wheel to re-tell the story in their own words using the present tense. For example:

1. It's the king's birthday.
2. The villagers want to give him some bread.
3. The villagers want to give him some bread and milk.
4. They decide to give him some honey.
5. Nora doesn't want to give him some honey.
6. She fills her cup with water.
7. The king arrives and tastes the honey pot.
8. The pot is full of water. The king is angry.

Follow-up

1 Ask the class to write the story of 'The Honey Pot' in their own words. This can be finished for homework if necessary.

2 Ask the pupils to read the stories to the class when they are finished and corrected.

Circle A

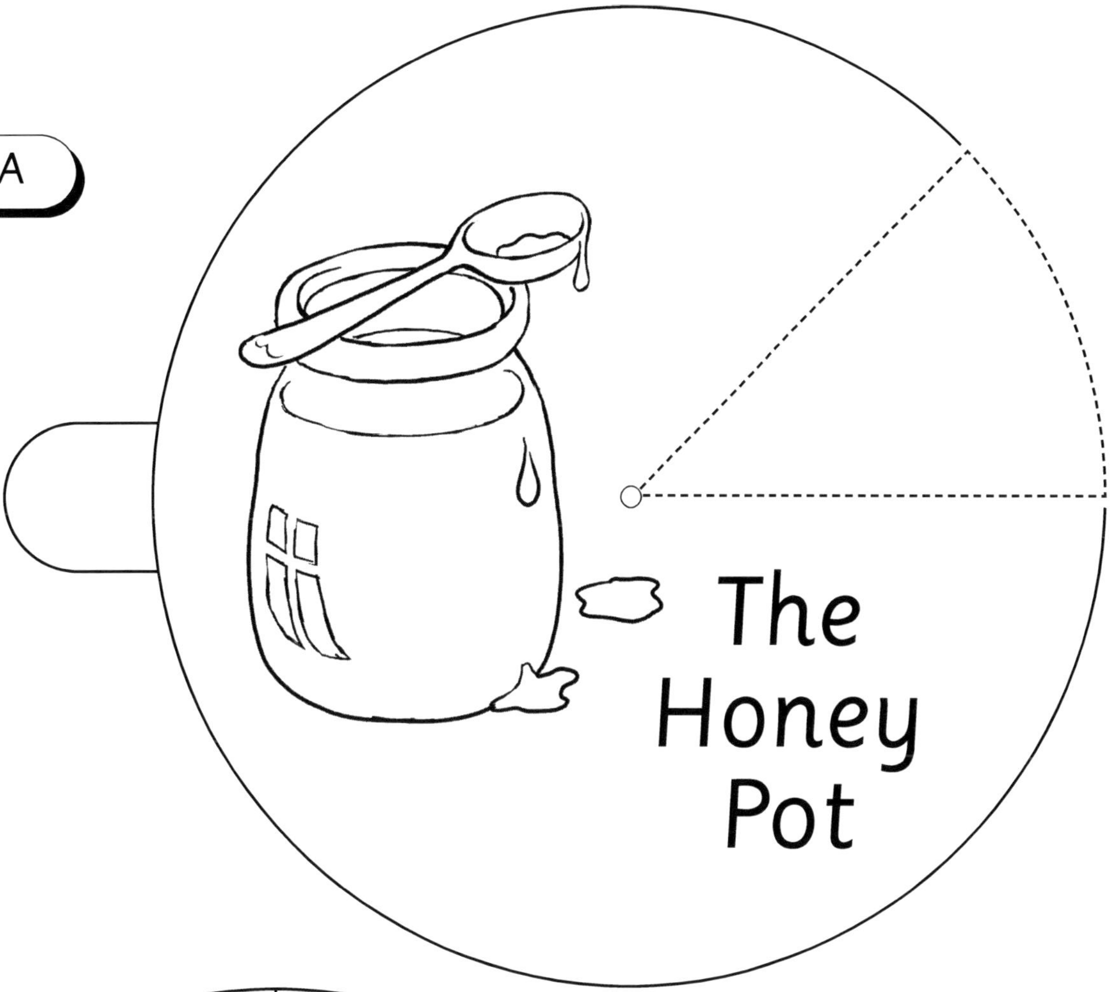

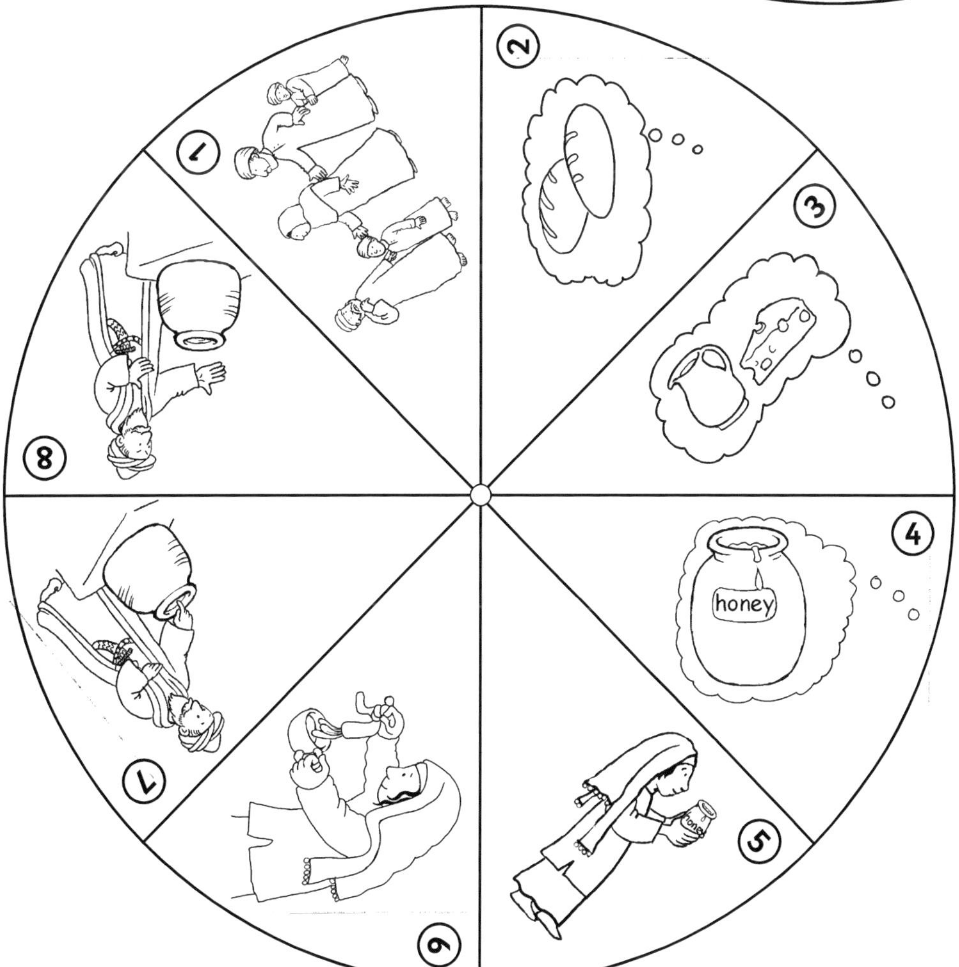

Circle B

Lesson 4

LISTENING
SPEAKING
READING
WRITING

Language

- regular past tense: *lived, loved, looked, opened, filled, watched, emptied, tasted, arrived, stared, asked, smiled, nodded, waited, shouted, wanted*

Materials

- a copy of Photocopiable page 69 per pair
- scissors, tooth picks
- coloured pencils/crayons

Warm-up

1 Write the past tense words above on the board.

2 Mime each action in turn and ask *What did I do?* Pupils answer *You nodded.*

3 Ask a pupil to come to the front of the class and mime an action, ask another pupil *What did he/she do?* This pupil answers then has a turn miming.

4 Divide the class into pairs A and B. Get them to take it in turns to mime and say the actions.

Procedure

1 Still in their pairs, give out copies of Photocopiable page 68.

2 Ask them to colour in the 2 bees a different colour each and also the spinner. They then cut these out and put a tooth pick through the hole in the centre of the spinner.

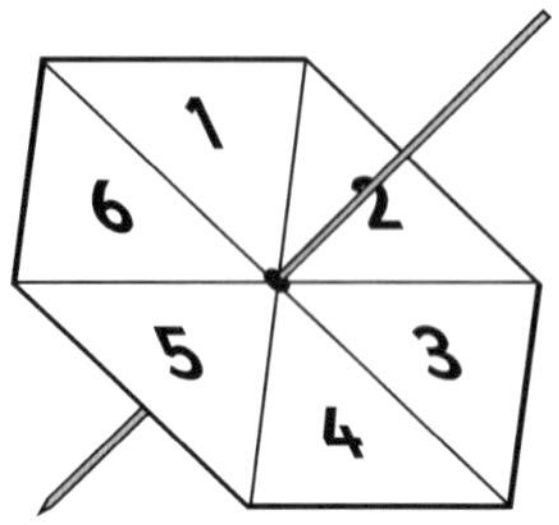

3 Explain that they must place their bees on START. Child A spins the spinner and moves along the relevant number of squares. They can move across or down the page. They must try to make up a sentence using the verb they land on. If it is correct they colour that square in. Go round helping to check sentences.

4 Child B now spins the spinner and moves the number of squares indicated. They also make a sentence and colour in the square using a different colour.

5 After a certain length of time, e.g. 20 minutes, ask the children to count how many words they have coloured in.

6 The child with the most words in correct sentences is the winner.

Follow-up

Ask the children to write 2/3 true sentences about what they did today using the verbs above.

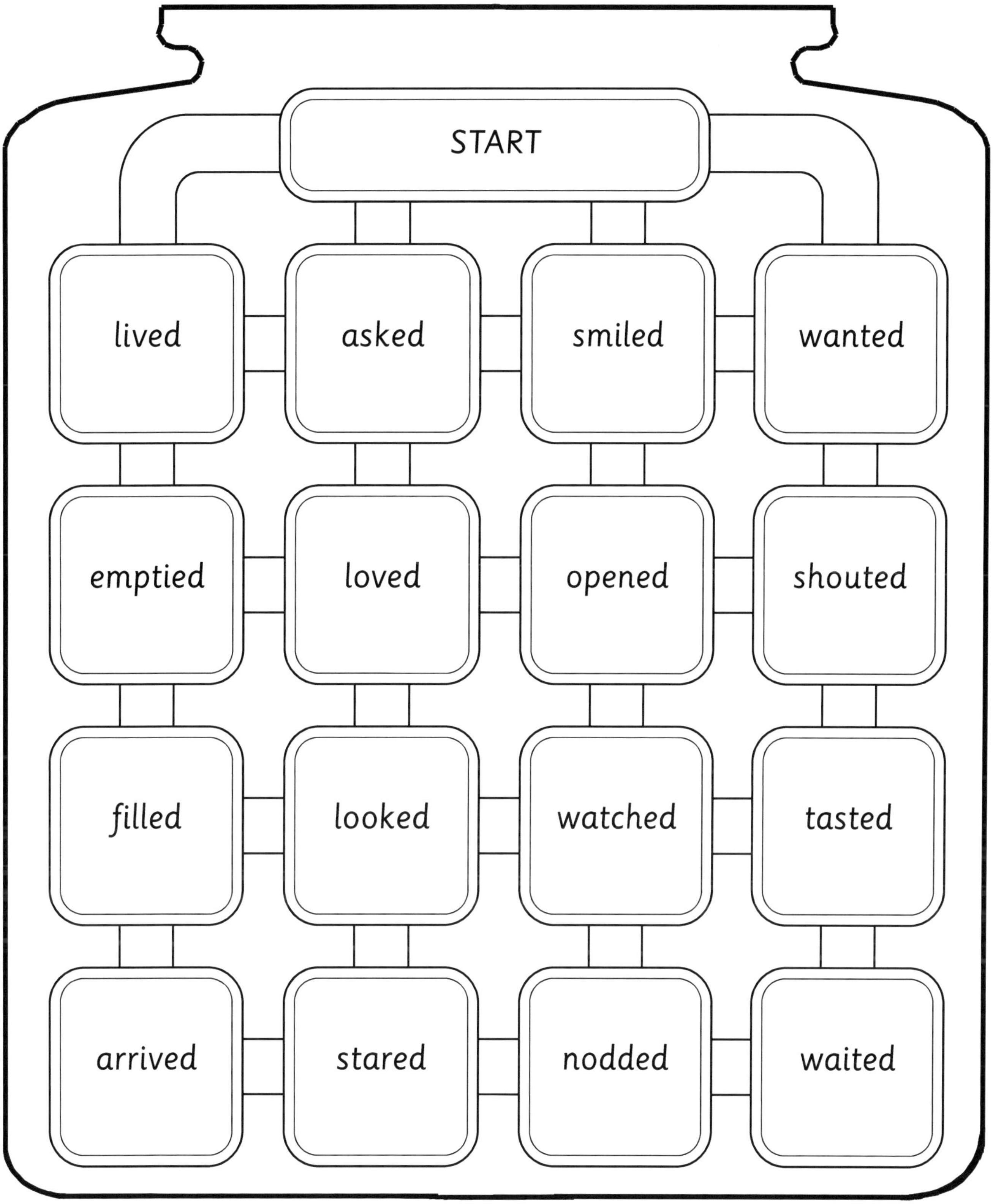
START
lived
asked
smiled
wanted
emptied
loved
opened
shouted
filled
looked
watched
tasted
arrived
stared
nodded
waited

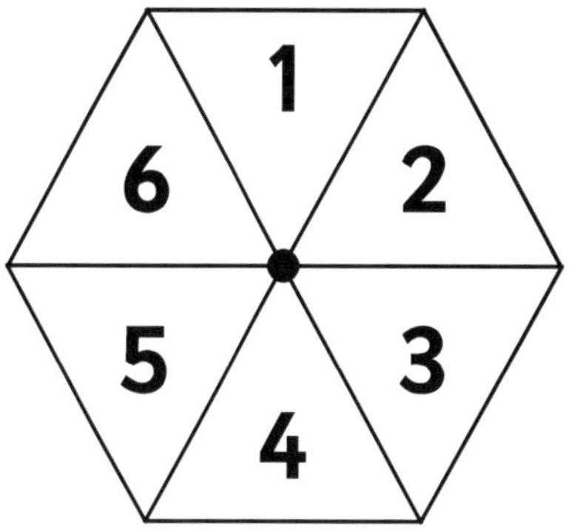
1
2
3
4
5
6

Lesson 5

LISTENING
SPEAKING
READING
WRITING

Language

- food vocabulary: *honey, bread, sausages, milk, cheese, eggs, biscuits, coffee, orange juice,* etc.
- ordinals: *first, second, third*

Materials

- a copy of Photocopiable page 71 per pupil
- coloured pencils /crayons
- glue
- scissors
- cassette

Warm-up

Ask the class *What do you think the king had for dinner on his birthday?* Elicit some new food vocabulary and include the words above. Ask them *What do you like for dinner?*

Procedure

1 Give out the copies of Photocopiable page 71. Ask the pupils to cut out the food items.

2 Play the cassette for the text below and tell the class to stick the correct item of food on the correct plate as they listen.

Tapescript

The king was very happy because it was his birthday. He had a special dinner with all the things he liked to eat. On the first plate he had sausages, eggs and milk. On the second plate he had orange juice with some bread and honey. Then on the third plate he had cheese, biscuits and a cup of coffee. He felt very full and a little bit ill!

3 Play the cassette again to make sure they have all put the items in the correct place.

4 Now ask *What did the king have on the first plate?* Repeat the question for the second and third plates.

Follow-up

Make a frieze for the classroom wall. Divide the class into six groups. Ask each group to draw one scene from the story (see below). They can write the words in speech bubbles above the heads of the characters:

Scene 1 Village scene with all the villagers discussing what to give the king for his birthday - a man suggests bread.

Scene 2 Villagers discussing what to give the king - a woman suggests milk and cheese.

Scene 3 Villagers still discussing the king's present - Nora suggests honey

Scene 4 Nora in the house filling her cup with water

Scene 5 Nora and villagers putting their cups into the large pot

Scene 6 Village scene with King tasting the liquid in the pot and being surprised/angry

Place the scenes in order on the classroom walls for all to see.

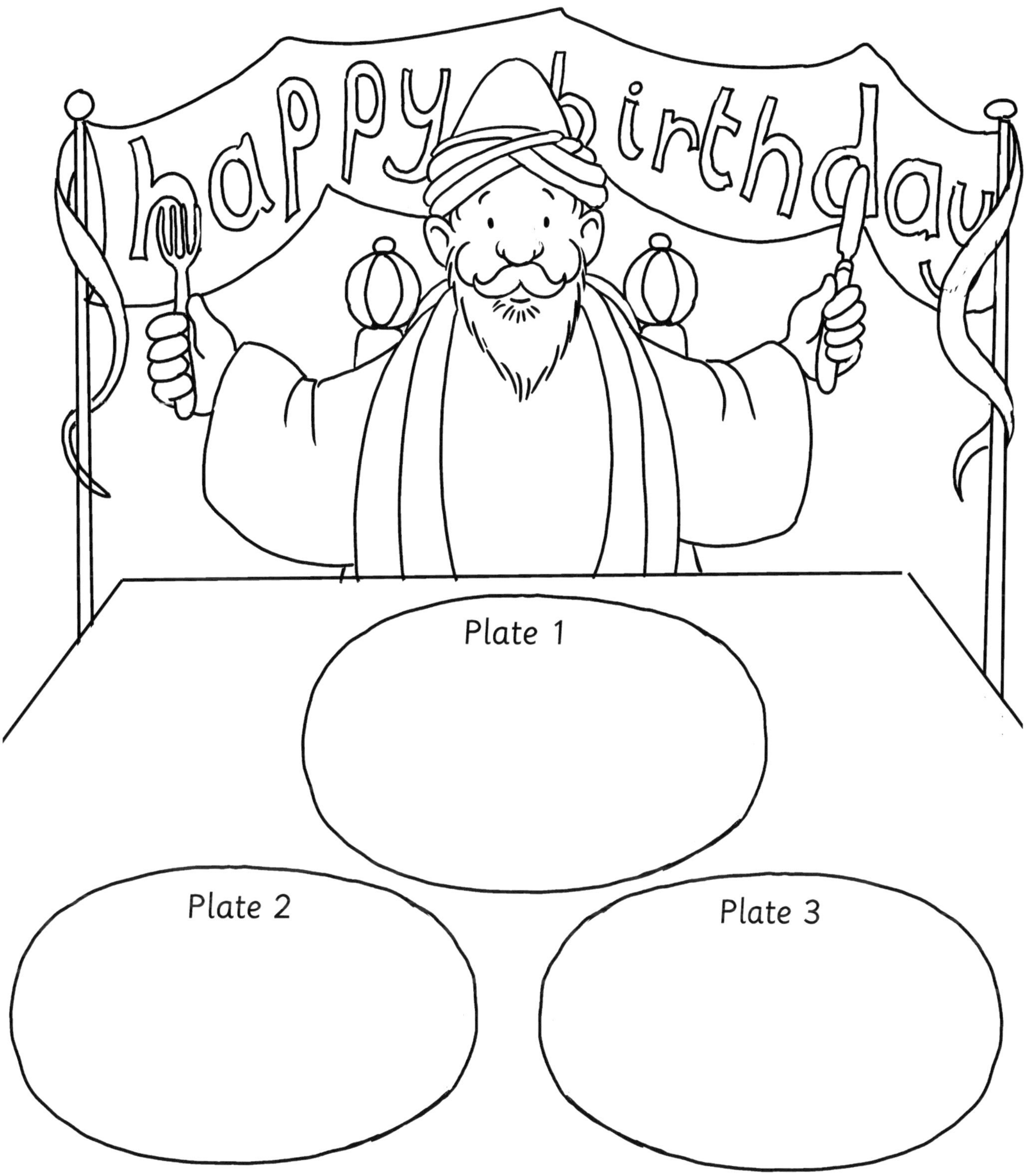
happy birthday
Plate 1
Plate 2
Plate 3

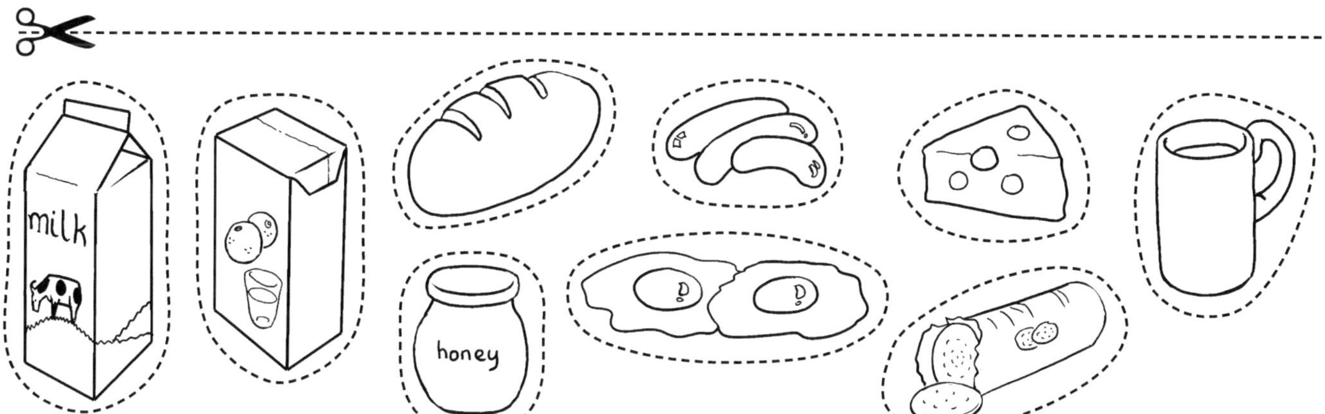
milk
honey

The Pied Piper

The people of Hamelin lived in a lovely old town with a river on one side and a mountain on the other.

All the people were very unhappy because the town was full of rats. There were rats in the streets. There were rats in the church and in the school. There were rats in the gardens and in the houses. There were rats in the bedrooms and rats in the kitchens. The people ran to the Mayor and said:

They fight the dogs
And scratch the cats
And bite the babies
And eat our hats
Run into our houses
And even get inside our trousers!

'Please, please stop the rats!' they cried.
'I am unhappy too. I don't like rats,' said the Mayor.

Just then a man came into town. He wore an old hat and a red and yellow jacket.
He carried a music pipe. He was called the Pied Piper.
'I can take your rats away for one hundred pounds,' he said.
'Oh, yes please!' cried the people.

The Pied Piper played his pipe and all the rats followed him.

They ran past the houses,

Past the church,

Past the shops,

Past the school,

Past the playground,

Through the market,

Over the bridge,

Around the pond,

Past the big tree,

Until they got to the river,

SPLASH!

They all fell in!

The people were very happy.
'Please can I have my money?' asked the Piper.
'No!' shouted the Mayor, 'go away!'
The Piper was very angry. He took out his pipe and played a different song.

Now all the children followed him.

They ran past the houses,
Past the church,
Past the shops,
Past the school,
Past the playground,
Through the market,
Over the bridge,
Around the pond,
Past the big tree,
Over the river,
And into the mountains.

The people of the town were very angry with the Mayor.

'You did not give the Piper his money,' they said, and they pushed the mayor into the river.

Then the Pied Piper played his pipe and they saw all the children running towards them.
'Thank you for our children,' the people said. 'Here is your hundred pounds.'

Then everyone had a wonderful party. They sang and ate wonderful food - and the mayor paid for everything!

Lesson 1

LISTENING
SPEAKING
READING
WRITING

Language

- story vocabulary
- present tense: *fight, scratch, bite, eat, run, get*
- past tense verbs: *was/were, ran, cried, said, fell, took, saw, had, came, wore*
- *What did … do?*

Materials

- cassette
- a copy of Photocopiable pages 72/73 per pair
- a copy of Photocopiable page 75 per pair
- a sheet of paper per pupil/ coloured pencils

Warm-up

Tell the children that this is a story about a town in Germany where, many years ago, there were far too many rats. The people were very unhappy.

Procedure

1 Give out the story on Photocopiable Pages 72/73 – one copy between two.

2 Ask the pupils to look at the pictures and answer questions like *What can you see? Where is the …? What is … doing/wearing?* etc.

3 Read the story to the children and point to the pictures. Ask some simple comprehension questions (in L1 if necessary) e.g. *What did the Pied Piper do?*

4 Play the cassette and stop after the chant in the box.

5 Ask the children to repeat the chant together as a class.

6 Then ask different pairs of children to say the chant, miming the actions if possible (e.g. fighting, scratching, biting).

Tapescript

They fight the dogs
And scratch the cats
And bite the babies
And eat our hats
Run into our houses
And even get inside our trousers!

7 Give out copies of Photocopiable page 75. Read through the sentences with the class. Then read the sentences while pupils point to the corresponding pictures.

8 Ask each pair to cut out their picture and sentence cards.

9 One pupil puts the pictures in a pile face down, and the other spreads the sentence cards face up on the desk.

10 Pupil 1 holds up picture card. Pupil 2 find the corresponding sentence. When all the cards have been paired, pupils change over. Go round checking to make sure they have matching pairs.

Follow-up

1 Explain to the children that the Pied Piper got his name because his clothes were divided into two colours.

2 Ask them to draw their own Pied Piper and to describe him/her to a partner, e.g. *My Pied Piper has yellow and red trousers and a green and blue shirt.*

3 They could then write a few sentences about him/her and stick these on the board with the pictures for other pupils to look at.

They fight the dogs.

They scratch the cats.

They bite the babies.

They eat our hats.

They run into our houses.

They get inside our trousers.

Lesson 2

LISTENING
SPEAKING
READING
WRITING

Language

- places: *house, church, shop, school, playground, market, bridge, pond, tree, river, mountain*
- verbs: *ran, got, fell*
- prepositions: *through, over, past, around*

Materials

- cassette
- a copy of Photocopiable pages 72/73 per pair
- a copy of Photocopiable page 77 per pupil

Warm-up

1 Ask the children: *Why were the people in the town so unhappy? (because of the rats). Who can take the rats away? (the Pied Piper).*

2 Pre-teach vocabulary. Give out copies of the story on Photocopiable pages 72/73. Play the cassette again and stop each time a place is mentioned, e.g. *house*, and ask pupils to point to a house in the story pictures. Continue with *shop, school* etc.

Procedure

1 Give out copies of Photocopiable page 77. Read or play the cassette for the rats' journey again, while pupils follow it on their map.

2 Ask them to complete part 1 by writing in the missing place names.

Answers: 1 church 2 shops
3 mountain 4 pond 5 tree
6 playground

3 To complete part 2 tell the children they are going to draw the rats' route to the river, preferably using a coloured pencil/pen.

4 Play the cassette for the journey again while pupils draw.

5 Check their answers by getting individual pupils to describe parts of the route.

Tapescript

They ran past the houses,
Past the church,
Past the shops,
Past the school,
Past the playground,
Through the market,
Over the bridge,
Around the pond,
Past the big tree,
Until they got to the river,
SPLASH!
They all fell in!

Follow-up

Ask pupils how they get to school. *Do they walk or go by bus? What do they go past? Do they go past a church? Do they go over a bridge?* etc. If you have time, or for homework, they could draw a simple map of their route from home to school. They can then describe this to a partner or to the class.

① Write in the missing places.

church shops pond tree playground mountain

② Draw the route the rats took.

Lesson 3

LISTENING
SPEAKING
READING
WRITING

Language

- story vocabulary
- past tense regular verbs: *followed, played*
- past tense irregular verbs: *fell, took, came, wore, was, were, ate, had*

Materials

- cassette (optional)
- a copy of Photocopiable page 79 per pupil
- scissors, pins

Warm-up

1 Write the present tense of the above verbs on the board. Get individual pupils to tell you the corresponding past tenses and write them on the board too.

2 Revise the story by asking questions like: *Who was unhappy? Who came into the town? What did he wear? Who fell in the river? What did the people have/eat?*

Procedure

1 Give out copies of Photocopiable page 79.

2 Tell the children to complete the first part by writing numbers in the boxes to put the story in the correct order.

3 They should be able to do this from memory, but if not play the cassette for the story again.

4 Check answers by asking individual pupils *What is picture/sentence 1?*

Answers: 1 c 2 f 3 a 4 d 5 e 6 b

Follow-up

Explain that they are going to play a game called 'Find Your Partner':

- The teacher cuts out the 12 sentence halves on Photocopiable page 79 and gives one sentence half to each pupil. (If you have more than 12 pupils in your class, you will have to photocopy the sentences and give out extra copies.)
- The pupils learn their phrase.
- Then pin the phrases on each of their backs.
- They now walk around their group saying their phrase to each other until they find the person who has the matching sentence half.

a The Pied Piper wore an old hat and a red and yellow jacket.

b Everyone had a wonderful party and they ate wonderful food.

c The people of Hamelin were unhappy because the town was full of rats.

d The Pied Piper played his pipe and the rats followed him.

e The pied Piper took out his pipe and played a different song.

f Just then a man came into town.

The Pied Piper wore	an old hat and a red and yellow jacket.
Everyone had a wonderful party	and they ate wonderful food.
The people of Hamelin were unhappy	because the town was full of rats.
The Pied Piper played his pipe	and the rats fell into the river.
The Pied Piper took out his pipe again	and the children followed him.
Just then a man	came into town.

Lesson 4

LISTENING
SPEAKING
READING
WRITING

Language

- irregular past tense: *was/were, get/got, eat/ate, run/ran, bite/bit, fight/fought, have/had, do/did*
- *What did I/he/it do?*

Materials

- a copy of Photocopiable page 81 per pupil
- scissors, sheet of paper
- cassette

Warm-up

1 Play the cassette for the chant again. Get pupils to chant it together.

2 Ask the pupils: *What did the rats eat? What did they fight?* etc.

Procedure

1 Give out copies of Photocopiable page 81.

2 Give out a sheet of A4 paper to each pupil. Get them to cut out 12 small rectangles to make 12 blank cards.

3 Tell the class that they are going to play Bingo with these cards. They each choose four verbs and cover them with 4 blank cards.

4 Choose one of the verbs (present or past) and say it out loud.

5 If a pupil has the corresponding word still showing on their bingo card they put a blank card on it.

6 Continue with other verbs at random.

7 The first pupil to shout *Bingo* when all their verbs are covered is the winner.

8 Pupils complete the bottom half of Photocopiable page 81 by writing in the missing past tense. They could do this in pairs or for homework.

Follow-up

Play a variation on the above game: pupils make up their own bingo card which contains 12 **past** tenses (any of the verbs appearing in the story). The teacher then calls out the **present** tense of the verbs and pupils cover the corresponding past tense if they have it. The first pupil to get 9 verbs covered shouts *bingo* and is the winner.

get	got	are	were
eat	ate	run	ran
bite	bit	fight	fought
have	had	do	did

had fought ate bit got did were ran

1 The people .... very unhappy.

2 The children .... into the mountains.

3 The rats .... the babies.

4 They .... the dogs.

5 The people .... a wonderful party.

6 The rats .... into the trousers.

7 They .... the hats.

8 The mayor .... not give the Pied Piper his money.

Lesson 5

LISTENING
SPEAKING
READING
WRITING

Language

- past tense: *there was/were*
- places vocabulary
- numbers 1–15

Materials

- a copy of Photocopiable page 83 per pair
- cassette

Warm-up

1 Ask the class to say the chant from the story.

2 Get them to change the verbs into the past tense and write it down on the board.

3 Then get them to say this new chant.

New chant

They fought the dogs
And scratched the cats
And bit the babies
And ate our hats
Ran into our houses
And even got inside our trousers!

Procedure

1 Give out copies of Photocopiable page 83 per pair. Point to each place and ask *What is this? It's a house.*

2 Give pupils a time limit and ask them to count and memorise how many rats they can see.

3 They then cover the picture with a sheet of paper and answer the questions below (working in their pairs).

4 Check their answers by getting individual pupils to say, e.g. *There were 15 rats in the house.*

Answers
House - 15
School - 1
Playground - 12
Tree - 4
Church - 6
River - 8
Total number of rats - 46

Follow-up

To finish off the work done on this story, the pupils could act it out.

Divide the class into: narrator (you could have more than one), people, children, rats, mayor, Pied Piper. The main characters practise their lines. The children/rats practise miming actions e.g. fighting, following the Pied Piper. Rehearse it a few times. If possible make/get costumes (e.g. Pied Piper could have a cloak and a flute; rats could have small masks). Perform the play in front of another class if possible.

How many rats were in the ...?

tree ☐ school ☐ church ☐ river ☐ house ☐ playground ☐

Total number of rats ☐

TELLING TALES *in English*

Photocopiable stories and activities for young learners

Written by Wendy Superfine and Megan James
Edited by Karen Gray
Designed by Christine Cox
Artwork by Tim Archbold, Pat Murray and Sarah Wimperis of GCI

1st edition 1 5 4 3 2 | 2022 21 20 19 18

The last figure shown denotes the year of impression.

Delta Publishing, 2003
www.deltapublishing.co.uk
www.klett-sprachen.de/delta

Printed in Germany

ISBN 978-3-12-501728-3